The Boat Beneath the Pyramid

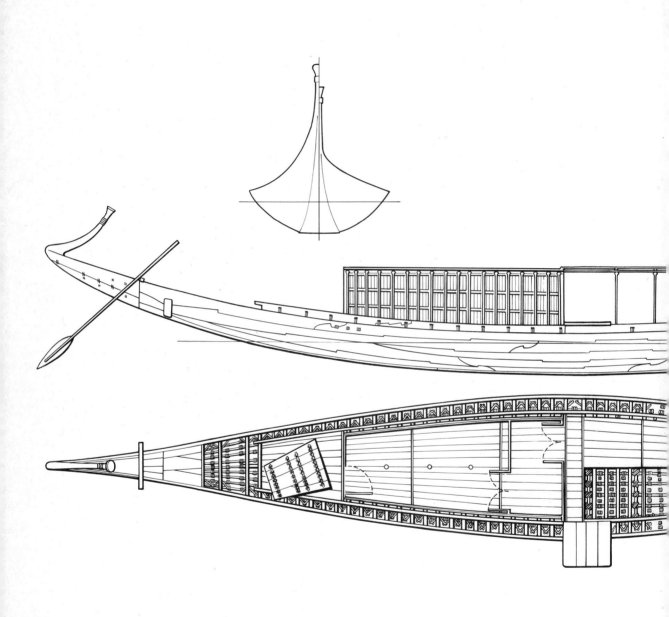

Nancy Jenkins

The Boat Beneath the Pyramid

King Cheops' Royal Ship

Special Consultant:
Ahmed Youssef Moustafa

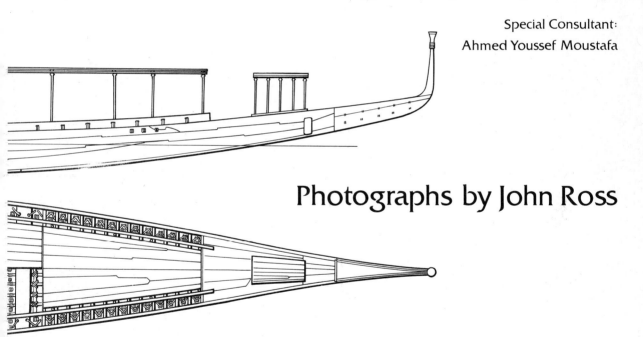

Photographs by John Ross

Holt, Rinehart and Winston
New York

For Sara and Nicholas, with thanks

Title-pages: *The reconstructed Royal Ship of Cheops (bow to the right), shown in section and plan views.*

First published in the United States of America in 1980 by Holt, Rinehart and Winston, 383 Madison Avenue, New York, New York 10017.

Library of Congress Cataloging in Publication Data
Jenkins, Nancy.
  The boat beneath the pyramid.

  Bibliography: p.
  Includes index.
  1. Ships, Wooden. 2. Cheops, King of Egypt – Tomb.
3. Giza. Great Pyramid of Cheops. 4. Egypt – Civilization – To 332 B.C. 5. Egypt – Religion. 6. Ships (in religion, folk-lore, etc) – Egypt. I. Title.
DT62.S55J46 1980   932'.01   79–27466

ISBN 0–03–057061–1

Printed and bound in Great Britain by Butler & Tanner Limited, Frome and London. Colour plates printed in Great Britain by Balding & Mansell Limited, Wisbech, Cambs.

Contents

Chronological table

BC	THE THIRTY-ONE DYNASTIES	BC	OLD KINGDOM	BC	THIRD & FOURTH DYNASTIES (principal rulers)
	Prehistory (Naqada II c. 3400)				
3150		2700		2700	
	Archaic Period Dyn. 1 and 2		Third Dynasty		Zoser (reigned 19 yrs.)
2700					
	Old Kingdom Dyn. 3–6	2630			
2250			Fourth Dynasty		
	1st Intermediate Period				Huni (24 yrs.)
2035		2520		2630	
	Middle Kingdom Dyn. 11–13				Sneferu (24 yrs.)
1668			Fifth Dynasty		Cheops (23 yrs.)
	2nd Intermediate Period				
1550					Djedefre (8 yrs.)
	New Kingdom Dyn. 18–20	2400			Chephren (? 25 yrs.)
946					Mycerinus (28 yrs.)
	Late Dynastic Period Dyn. 21–31		Sixth Dynasty		Shepseskaf (5 yrs.)
					Khentkawes (?)
332		2250		2520	

Note: There is still considerable disagreement among scholars as to the precise chronology for ancient Egypt and dates are therefore only approximate. The system adopted here follows that proposed by the Oriental Institute, University of Chicago. The tinted area indicates the period of main relevance for this book.

CHAPTER ONE

Introduction

Shem el-Nessim is an ancient Egyptian festival that goes back at least to Ptolemaic times and probably even earlier, the one feast in the crowded Egyptian holiday calendar that unites in celebration the stark and divisive elements of the country – young and old, male and female, rich and poor, Muslim, Copt, Greek, and Jew. Shem el-Nessim means 'the sniffing of the breezes' and that is precisely what everyone does, the entire populace rushing out of doors on the First of May for a last breath of fresh air before the hammer of summer's heat stuns the country into silent, submissive lethargy.

The rich desert the city to celebrate the holiday on their country estates and the bourgeoisie dance and feast in the poolside gardens of foreign hotels. But, for the impoverished mass of Cairo's population – those who can afford nothing more than the few piastres it costs for a whole family to crowd on the ramshackle city buses – a holiday of this sort means an outing along the narrow, littered stretch of river bank that lies between the coffee-coloured surge of the Nile and the traffic streaming along the riverside corniche behind.

Along the bank, women are cooking holiday feasts, while Arab music drones from transistor radios and young men beat an accompaniment on finger drums. The pungent smell of charcoal fires and roasting spiced meat and garbage-dung-rotting fruit mingles with something rich and dark and loamy from the river itself. The sun, dipping towards the palms on the distant Giza shore, flushes the Nile with a sheen like peach-coloured metal. Feluccas flick back and forth in the stiff breeze, their lateen sails dipping perilously in the relentless northward fall of the river. Overladen vaporetti, the little motor launches that transport Cairenes from one end to another of their great city, ply the current, while rowboats, in unskilled hands, spin like helpless waterbugs on the surface and occasionally capsize. The thronging crowds, the sounds, the smells, the sense of a chaotic release of energies that have been pent up by the strictures of poverty and religion alike, are overwhelming. So often in Egypt one has this sense of the magic

of an event that is powerfully ancient and, despite its secular aspects, profoundly religious, as charged with emotions as an ancient rite. This is a country, one feels, that is riveted in the past, its strengths and weaknesses both derived from a hypnotic fixation on three thousand years of history that ended before the birth of Christ.

I was there in Cairo during Shem el-Nessim to see an ancient boat, the oldest boat in the world, and one which, many historians and archaeologists believe, may once have floated on this same Nile, perhaps in a festival as joyous and emotional as the one I was witnessing. Not just the oldest boat in the world, it is also the largest and the best-preserved ancient boat known to archaeology, a graceful and elegant construction, nearly forty-five metres long from stem to stern, and solidly built of cedar from the distant mountains of the Lebanon. It is an important source of information about the ancient origins of ship-building and a work of art as austerely impressive as the pyramid it was built to complement.

The boat's discovery dates to 1954, when two massive sealed pits were found beneath a pile of rubble just south of the Great Pyramid of Giza. Carved into the limestone bedrock of the Giza plateau, the two pits, it seemed obvious, formed part of the funerary complex of the Great Pyramid, the pyramid of King Cheops, second ruler of the Fourth Dynasty of the Egyptian Old Kingdom, king of Upper and Lower Egypt around the middle of the third millennium B C.

1 When one of the pits was opened, inside it were found the remains of this ancient boat, its timbers dismantled, and its 651 separate parts carefully arranged in thirteen layers, one over the other, exactly as they had been placed some four and a half millennia earlier, presumably at the same time that King Cheops himself was buried in his tomb in the heart of the adjacent pyramid. Incredibly, when they were removed from the pit, the dismantled timbers were found to be almost perfectly preserved. Years

1 A composite photograph of the dismantled ship, taken shortly after the forty-one blocks covering the pit had been removed. The papyriform prow can be seen at the left-hand or western end. Fragments of white plaster that had fallen into the pit in ancient times are distributed over the surface.

of patient, diligent and meticulous work followed before the great ship was returned to its original splendour. The work was largely that of one man, Ahmed Youssef Moustafa, Chief Restorer of the Egyptian Department of Antiquities and a man who is almost legendary for his skill and perspicacity in the demanding field of the restoration of antiquities.

Today Hag Ahmed Youssef, as he has been known since his hajj-pilgrimage to Mecca in 1935, is the zealous and watchful custodian of the boat. A short, robust man in his late sixties, he is a devout and orthodox Muslim whose spirited intelligence and humour are reflected in clear, dark brown eyes. He divides most of his time between the museum that was built next to the Great Pyramid in the 1960s to house the boat, and the bungalow provided for him by the Department of Antiquities, a small but comfortable mud-brick rest-house situated in a low desert wadi between the pyramid plateau and the modern village of Kfar es-Sammân below. On that warm and windy May afternoon, when all Egypt was celebrating Shem el-Nessim, I had driven out to the pyramids to meet the Hag and, I hoped, finally to see the great ship. I had visited and talked with Hag Ahmed often over the past months but always there was some reason why I could not be admitted to the museum. Permission must come from the Department of Antiquities; it is rarely given and all visitors must be accompanied by Hag Ahmed who takes frank pleasure in these rare opportunities to show off his treasure. That day, an archaeologically minded Pakistani general on an official visit to Egypt had been given permission to see the boat. Through an intermediary, the Hag had let me know that I might slip in with the official party.

8

2 The Nile in flood at Giza – a photograph taken in the late 1920s. Because the climate is almost totally rainless, before the completion of the Aswan High Dam agriculture in Egypt depended on the regular, annual summer flood of the Nile. The dramatic – and romantic – spectacle is, alas, a thing of the past and Egypt today relies on irrigation for her needs. The village of Kfar es-Sammân, at the foot of the Giza plateau, marks the edge of cultivation. Beneath the modern town lie the remains of Cheops' valley temple.

From certain parts of Cairo, the three Giza pyramids appear across the flat reach of the Nile like three perfect and slightly incongruous alps, hovering on the desert's edge beyond the dust and smoke of the city. The approach to the pyramids is along a modern dual carriageway that runs between depressing rows of cheap nightclubs and squat, ugly apartment blocks right up to the very foot of the escarpment. Desert dust and traffic fumes darken the air and choke the palms and gum trees that line the roadside. It is hard to deny the majesty of the pyramid site, rising impressively above the rather squalid surroundings, yet harder still to imagine what it must have been like even as recently as fifty years ago when the

2 Nile in flood reached to the village of Kfar es-Sammân just under the pyramid plateau, and the imposing bulk of the monuments was mirrored in the placid surface of the floodwaters. It must have been easier in those days to picture what ancient Egypt was like. Today modern Egypt, noisy, dirty, exuberant, bursting with vitality, intrudes on the romantic imagination.

10

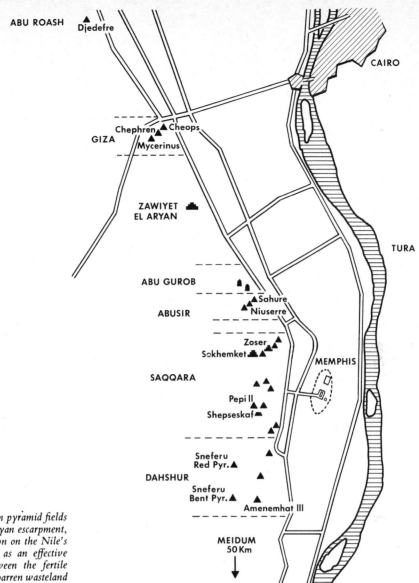

ABU ROASH
Djedefre

CAIRO

GIZA
Chephren ▲ Cheops
Mycerinus

ZAWIYET
EL ARYAN

TURA

ABU GUROB

Sahure
ABUSIR
Niuserre

Zoser
Sekhemket

MEMPHIS

SAQQARA

Pepi II
Shepseskaf

Sneferu
Red Pyr. ▲
DAHSHUR

Sneferu
Bent Pyr. ▲
Amenemhat III

MEIDUM
50 Km

*3 The Old Kingdom pyramid fields
stretch along the Libyan escarpment,
an irregular formation on the Nile's
west bank that acts as an effective
natural barrier between the fertile
river valley and the barren wasteland
of the western desert.*

    All told, there are some eighty pyramids now known in Egypt, *3*
scattered in a long irregular line along the west bank of the Nile, with
most of them concentrated in the area between Abu Roash, just north
of Giza, and the Faiyum depression, near which the rulers of the Middle
Kingdom erected their monuments. Nonetheless, mention of 'the pyramids' unfailingly calls to mind for most people this group on the Giza
plateau, without doubt the most familiar group of monuments in the *II, 14*
entire world. The Great Pyramid of King Cheops (or Khufu, as he is less *I*
popularly but more properly known), is the largest and oldest of these.
Next comes the middle pyramid, that of King Chephren, or Khafre, one

of Cheops' sons; it is in fact shorter than Cheops' pyramid by about seventy-five centimetres, though because it lies on higher ground from some aspects it appears to dominate the earlier one. The pyramid of Mycerinus, or Menkaure, probably a grandson of Cheops, is the smallest of the three. The pyramids of Mycerinus and Cheops are each accompanied by three smaller, subsidiary pyramids, said to have been built for the principal queens of these two kings, so that the whole Giza 'pyramid field', as Egyptologists call it, in fact comprises nine pyramids.

From Hag Ahmed's rest-house to the museum, it is a short walk, up the causeway whose ancient paving stones still lead from the valley to the Chephren pyramid, and behind a group of Old Kingdom mastabas, the large, rectangular tombs that were erected around the pyramids for nobles and court officials. The Great Pyramid, Hag Ahmed explained, as we walked along the causeway, was the first to be built on the Giza plateau. Earlier kings, such as Cheops' father Sneferu (who may have had as many as three pyramids), had erected their monuments farther south, near the Old Kingdom capital of Memphis, now lost amid the canals and marshes on the west bank of the river, across from the modern industrial site of Helwan. Indeed, with the northerly breeze clearing the desert air, we could see the great pyramid fields extending away to the south: the later Fifth Dynasty constructions at Abusir; the Step Pyramid of King Zoser, earliest of all known pyramid-builders, at Saqqara; and, in the blue distance, the Red Pyramid and the unmistakable rhomboid shape of the Bent Pyramid, both at Dahshur and both apparently built by Sneferu. Why Cheops decided to erect his pyramid so much farther north than the others is one of those questions that Egyptologists may never answer, but perhaps the splendid isolation of the site lent itself to the kind of imposing nature that Cheops wanted for his burial.★

4   The glass-walled museum that houses Cheops' great boat was erected just south of the Great Pyramid and directly over the now empty pit in which the boat was found – although displayed is an inappropriate word to use, for it is a museum that no tourist is permitted to visit and few students have even been inside. The museum, I had been assured by experts in the field, is a disaster in its desert location, its glass walls and roof producing extremes of temperature and humidity that subject the ship's timbers to unbearable stresses and make the future of the boat uncertain.

★ That isolation was not to last long. Although Cheops' son and successor Djedefre built the most northerly pyramid of all, a now ruined heap of stones at Abu Roash, about five miles north of Giza, *his* successor, Chephren, returned to his father's site and only a few years later erected the second pyramid there.

4 *The southern side of the Great Pyramid of Cheops, showing the modern museum in the foreground that today houses the Royal Ship.*

As we went through the little museum, examining photographs, drawings, models, exhibits of haphazardly coiled ropes and matting that had once covered the dismantled timbers, Hag Ahmed explained the steps of his excavation and reconstruction, a process that in the end took him about sixteen years. In fact, it was not until 1970 that the ship was reassembled *93* in the museum – finally, after a number of false starts, erected on its present site over the pit.

I had been impressed before, in reading and talking with Hag Ahmed, by the age and size of the ship; but I was quite unprepared for its tremendous aesthetic impact. The ancient cedar timbers are darkly glowing, their warm, resinous perfume pervading the dusty air of the museum. The deep sheer of the boat's profile is quite extraordinarily beautiful, with its high *V* prow and steeply raked stern pieces derived from the ancient papyrus reed rafts that must have been the first Egyptian method of transportation. To the pure lines and the majestic concept is united a fineness and delicacy of detail that is so typical of this Fourth Dynasty civilization – a character

13

revealed not only in the exquisitely carved papyrus-bud and palmiform finials of the canopy's slender columns, but also in a detail as prosaic as

5–7 a door handle. These three characteristics – purity, majesty, delicacy – return again and again, in stone sculpture, in architecture, even in the fragments of painted and carved relief that we know from the period. The Fourth Dynasty set the stamp, as it were, on Egyptian civilization, establishing the classical canons to which later generations would turn. It is an important point to remember in our consideration of the Cheops boat, whether we think of it as an aesthetic object, a religious or ritual symbol, or indeed from the point of view of pure functionalism.

Air conditioning to control the temperature and humidity is not available in the museum; the reasons given are various, but the one that makes most sense is that there is simply insufficient electric power on the plateau to run the huge refrigerating unit that sits rusting outside the museum building. Why the available power cannot be stepped up is another question, but questions like this are a source of deep embarrassment to the Egyptian government which seems singularly helpless and peculiarly unable to do anything about it. Time and again, when I asked foreign archaeologists, Egyptologists or museum people about the ship, my questions would begin, 'Well, why don't they just . . . ?' And the reply always came back, with a remote smile, 'Ah, you see, you don't know Egypt.' Hag Ahmed monitors the ship carefully, but without the proper equipment there is little he can do to protect it, devoted though he is to its well-being. Cheops' Royal Ship has survived for more than 4,500 years, but serious doubts have been raised whether it will remain intact even for another decade unless drastic measures are taken to rescue it.

What the huge vessel was, what function or functions it was built to serve, are questions that have puzzled archaeologists and historians since its discovery. Some Egyptologists have called the ship a Solar Barque, a boat to carry the dead king of Egypt, resurrected and floating with the Sun-god on his eternal round across the sky; others say it was a funerary barge, to carry the king's embalmed body down-river from Memphis, the Old Kingdom capital, to Giza for burial in the pyramid he had spent his life building; still others call it a pilgrimage boat, used in the king's own lifetime to visit the holy places of Egypt, or for his other-worldly pilgrimages in the hereafter. I prefer to follow Björn Landström, the Swedish expert on ancient boats, and call it the 'Royal Ship' of Cheops, for royal it most certainly was, and as for its other uses and functions, these are not yet known for certain.

Apart from official excavation reports and a few scholarly articles of interest only to Egyptologists, nothing has been published previously about the Royal Ship of Cheops. Landström, in his exhaustive catalogue

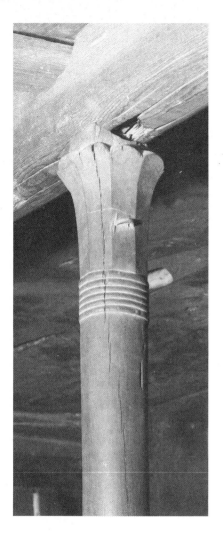

5–7 Purity and restraint together with a superb technical finish were the hallmarks of Fourth Dynasty craftsmanship, as is evident from these few details from the Royal Ship – a palmiform column supporting the cabin roofbeam, a door latch perhaps carved deliberately to evoke the scarab beetle sacred to the Egyptians, and a sliding lock that is both elegant and economic. Note the copper brads, one on the column and several on the lock, that are among the few instances of the use of metal in the Royal Ship.

of ancient Egyptian boats, *Ships of the Pharaohs* (1970), discussed the Royal Ship, but his scope was too vast to include more than a brief mention, and although his insights into the ship's construction are invaluable, it seems important to understand the ship as something more than the product of the ancient shipwright's craft. For it was also the product of a civilization, one of the highest civilizations in man's long history, as well as one of the most ancient. That rapid flowering of culture that was the Pyramid Age not only set the pattern for the millennia of Egyptian civilization that were to follow; it also created, in art, in literature, in architecture, and, as we now see, in ship-building, works, monuments and objects that would stun future generations with their technological proficiency as much as their artistic perfection. Achievement of this order did not spring forth fully blown in the Fourth Dynasty. Centuries of development must lie behind the grace, the strength, the assurance of the craft. No less than the pyramids, the Royal Ship is a testimony to the advanced civilization that built it.

The sun had set when we left the museum that day, and the holiday-makers had long since departed. The wind had dropped; already a night-time chill had begun to creep into the air. In the brief desert twilight the pyramids stood out in all their ruined majesty, dark hulks that loomed against the last apricot-coloured glow in the western sky. At night the Giza plateau is a lonely place, cold and forbidding, inhabited only by a few guards, wrapped like mummies against the night wind, and the yapping, threatening pi-dogs of Egypt.

From a time long before King Cheops this plateau had been a sacred burying ground, and even today there is about it a sense of holiness and mystery, especially in the empty silences of the night. The ancient people who built these monuments, and apparently buried their kings within, are in a way as mysterious to us as the pyramids themselves. Who built them, who equipped them with great boats on the magnificent scale of Cheops' Royal Ship, and how and why this happened, are questions that we must find answers to, however tentative. But we cannot begin to understand the Royal Ship, its design, its function and the reasons why it was buried so carefully in its pit next to the Great Pyramid, until we understand more about the civilization that built it and what that civilization thought of itself and its world.

8 *Ahmed Youssef Moustafa, who restored and reconstructed the Royal Ship of Cheops.*

9 This little ivory statuette, just five centimetres high, is the only known portrait of King Cheops. It was found in the Temple of Khentiamentiu, Lord of the Westerners as the dead were called, at the holy city of Abydos.

CHAPTER TWO

The pyramid-builders

The Egyptians were among the first people in the world to develop a written language. By the year 3000 BC, some five hundred years before the ascent of King Cheops to the throne, the hieroglyphic script and the language it expressed had evolved the basic forms they would preserve – though subject to great changes in vocabulary, grammar and orthography – for more than three thousand years. (The latest hieroglyphs so far discovered, from the island of Philae at Aswan, are dated to the year AD 394, well into the Christian era.) Thus the Egyptians were also among the first people to preserve a record of historical events. The farther back in history one goes, of course, the more shadowy becomes that record; yet we probably know more about the early Egyptians than we do about any other ancient people.

The Sumerians of Lower Mesopotamia had also developed an early writing system at about the same time as the Egyptians, but they lacked the other factor that contributes so much to our knowledge of Egypt – the factor of climate. The hot, dry sands of the desert preserve whatever is buried in them and, probably for this very reason, they were selected by the Egyptians as the location of their burying grounds.

Nonetheless, for all the historical records and the preserved artefacts, we still know little about ancient Egyptian history and civilization. Part of this has to do with the reticence of the ancient chroniclers on the very subjects that we find fascinating. Their ideas of what constituted an event worthy of historical mention are seldom the same as our own. Much of the ancient record is given over to prayers and offering formulas that vary little from one generation to another. From the period of the Old Kingdom, which lasted five hundred years, our knowledge is further limited by the fact that we have nothing but burials to go on. There are no remains of cities, no domestic architecture, no settlement patterns, until a much later period. This gives us a curiously one-sided perception of the ancient Egyptians as a peculiarly morbid people, obsessed by death. While it is true, as we shall see, that the fact of death was a focus of their

10 *The slate palette of Narmer is the most important of a series of these ritual objects used for the preparation of cosmetics and body paint, and dating from late predynastic and early dynastic times. Crowned by heads of the cow-goddess Hathor, the palette shows on the reverse King Narmer wearing the White Crown of Upper Egypt in the characteristic pharaonic pose, subduing his enemies. On the obverse the king, in the topmost register, wears the Red Crown of Lower Egypt while his decapitated enemies lie before him. Narmer has been identified with the legendary King Menes, who unified the Two Lands. Note on the obverse the little papyriform boat in the upper right-hand corner.*

civilization, there is also solid evidence that they were a gay and life-loving people, not so very different from their present-day descendants in the Nile Valley.

The date 3000 BC is significant. The art of writing cannot have sprung forth fully developed in that year; it had a long evolution that can only be traced in part, and it continued to evolve long after that date. Nonetheless, something very important happened in Egypt around the beginning of the third millennium. Precisely what the events were and in what sequence they took place is not at all clear. Writing developed as a tool of communication for the small but powerful educated class at the same time as a political event of the first order occurred: the unification of Upper and Lower Egypt with a new capital at Memphis, the walls of

10   which were traced, according to a well-established tradition, by Menes, first king of the First Dynasty. The unification of the Nile Valley under one ruler, the establishment of the First Dynasty, and the 'invention' of writing are all related and interdependent events. An important factor

in the strength and stability of the new political order must have been the ability to communicate, by means of the written word and often over long distances, so that an edict, transcribed in Memphis and marked with the king's authenticating seal, could be transported by boat to Upper Egypt or the Delta or on foot to the eastern desert outposts and mining camps, and there carried out.

By the time of the Fourth Dynasty, which seems to have been established some time shortly before 2600 BC, the Old Kingdom Egyptians had evolved a highly advanced society with a technology that was sophisticated in the sense that they were able to achieve astounding feats of engineering with extremely primitive equipment. A strong centralized government was focused on the king, who was responsible in a very direct and immediate way for the fertility of the soil, which depended on the regular seasonal inundation when the Nile burst its banks and flooded the valley, depositing a layer of rich mud from the African highlands where the river has its source. On the fertility of the soil, of course, depended the survival of all Egypt, so that the king was in a real sense the guarantor of that survival, the mediator between the Egyptians and their gods (it appears that all offerings to the gods were made in the king's name alone), indeed probably a god himself. It was to house this god's immortal spirit and to nourish it through prayers and offerings that the pyramids were built.

The pyramids

As architectural achievements, the pyramids are awesome constructions; when one considers the limitations under which the Fourth Dynasty Egyptians operated, they are quite unbelievable. It would be another thousand years before Egyptians would know and use the wheel; they would not discover the block-and-tackle, or any lifting device more sophisticated than the simple lever, until the Roman period; their arithmetical computations were extremely awkward, based on a complicated system of doubling pairs of numbers and adding or subtracting the results, and they hardly knew compound fractions at all. Yet in just over a hundred years they built at least seven pyramids and perhaps completed an eighth. More than two million stones were used in the Great Pyramid alone; their average weight was two-and-a-half tons, and some blocks weighed fifteen tons. Much of the stone was quarried locally, but some of it was transported from as far away as distant Aswan, at the Nile's first *94* cataract in Upper Egypt.

And it was not just pyramids alone, for each of the main pyramids was the focus of a vast complex covering many acres of ground. On the edge *11*

21

of cultivation, at the high point reached by the Nile during its annual spate, stood the Valley Temple, with a landing stage for funerary and other boats, and a canal connecting it to the river to facilitate boat travel even at times of a low Nile. A high, walled Causeway led from the Valley Temple up to the pyramid on the Libyan plateau, an escarpment that runs along the west bank of the Nile for hundreds of miles. Against the east side of the pyramid the Mortuary Temple was built to face the rising sun. Inside the Mortuary Temple a 'false door', a recessed stone stela that was a characteristic part of all burial equipment, royal or otherwise, permitted the dead king to enter the temple from his tomb in the pyramid and partake of the daily offerings that were made to him here. A high temenos or boundary wall surrounded the pyramid area and restricted access to all but the ritually clean priests and officials who performed the daily services.

Within the pyramid complex, but usually outside the temenos wall, were subsidiary pyramids; the evidence is slender, but many archaeologists believe these to have been the intended burial places of the king's principal wives, or of his daughters. It is also possible that they were meant for the ceremonial interment of various royal paraphernalia, crowns, staves, maces and so forth. Most of the Fourth Dynasty pyramids also had boat-pits carved into the limestone bedrock of the plateau – it may indeed be discovered that *all* Fourth Dynasty pyramids had boat-pits, but whether they all originally contained boats, and whether those boats were of the magnificent size and scale of the Royal Ship, is not now known.

As well as engineering geniuses, the Egyptians had also to be superior organizers in order to erect and furnish these monuments. Dows Dunham

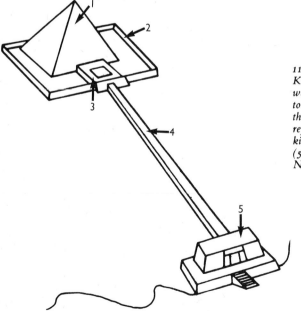

11 In the traditional arrangement of an Old Kingdom pyramid complex, the pyramid itself (1) was surrounded by a boundary or temenos wall (2) to seal off the sacred precinct. On the east side of the pyramid, the mortuary temple (3) served as the repository of daily offerings to maintain the dead king's spirit. A causeway (4) led to the valley temple (5) at the edge of cultivation and the height of the Nile in flood.

of the Boston Museum of Fine Arts has estimated that no more than 2,500 people could have worked on the pyramid's face at any one time. But there would also have been thousands more labourers in the quarry and transport crews, as well as the artists, sculptors, painters and skilled stone carvers who were responsible for the sumptuous decorations (coloured stones, painted reliefs, inscriptions, statues of the king and gods) that adorned these buildings – not to mention the supply crews (butchers, bakers, brewers, cooks) needed to keep the armies of workers provided with their daily rations.

The earliest Egyptian burials that we know of were shallow excavations in the desert sand where the body, wrapped in linen and accompanied by the simplest of grave-goods (jewelry, weapons, tools, offering jars), was laid. Gradually these simple pit-graves became more elaborate, lined with mud-brick and roofed with wood, and enlarged to contain several chambers. By the First Dynasty this simple type of pit-grave had evolved into the mastaba tomb, so-called because the low, rectangular super-structure over the burial is said to resemble the mastaba benches outside modern Upper Egyptian homes. The mastaba tomb of King Aha at Saq-qara, according to Walter Emery who excavated a number of First and Second Dynasty royal tombs there in the late 1930s and after, had twenty-seven small chambers in the mud-brick superstructure, each containing various kinds of offerings for the king's use in the other world. These offerings might be real, such as jewelry or jars of grain and oil, or they might be substitutes, models in a more durable, often more precious material to take the place of perishable items. Or they might be miniatures of offering objects that were too large or otherwise unsuitable for placing in the grave.

North of King Aha's imposing tomb, and situated in such a way that it seemed clearly to be part of the burial equipment, Emery found a boat-pit more than nineteen metres long with a brick superstructure 'crude enough to suggest that it was constructed after the boat had been put into position'. Fragments of wood and rope fibre found in this and other early boat-pits at Saqqara indicated to Emery that they had once actually con-tained real boats.

With each succeeding generation, these royal tombs became larger and more imposing, public declarations of the power of the god-king, un-diminished even in death, and surrounded by the graves of his nobles and courtiers. The first great architectural advance came in the Third Dynasty with the monumental use of stone as a building material. Stone had occa-sionally been used in the past for architectonic elements, such as lintels and door frames, but in the Step Pyramid built for King Zoser at Saqqara, *12* quarried stone blocks instead of mud-brick were used structurally for the first time in the massive complex, a six-stepped pyramid with courts and chapels surrounding it. The architectural advance indicates a change in the way of expressing the king's power, and possibly, although we have no way of knowing for sure, a change in the very nature of that power. No longer was the king's grave simply the largest among many similar graves; now the structure, and perhaps the purpose, of the grave was entirely different. The Step Pyramid dominated the necropolis; it was clearly visible from miles away, and especially from Memphis, the white-walled capital that lay in the green valley below the pyramid plateau. Moreover, with its great courts and temples and subsidiary buildings, the Step Pyramid represented an entirely different concept from King Aha's mastaba with its twenty-seven offering chambers; the Step Pyramid was both a residence for the divine spirit of the dead king, as grand as anything he had had in real life, and a sanctuary for continued worship and propitiation of the god, where offerings and rituals would be continued on a daily basis.

12 The Third Dynasty King Zoser's Step Pyramid at Saqqara, shown here in a model reconstruction, represents the first known example of the monumental use of stone in building. With its many temples and courtyards (including the hebsed-court inside the eastern wall for rituals at the king's jubilee), it is much more complicated than the pyramid complexes of the Fourth Dynasty.

13 *The name of King Cheops (or Khufu, to give him his proper designation), enclosed in the royal cartouche, has been found on limestone building blocks used in the now ruined pyramid of Amenemhet I at Lisht, indicating that the Twelfth Dynasty king had despoiled his predecessor's mortuary temple in order to erect his own funerary monument – and indicating too in how little regard the great Old Kingdom ruler was held by much later generations.*

The second great architectural advance came later in the Third Dynasty or early in the Fourth Dynasty, with the transition from a step pyramid to a true pyramid at Meidum. The now ruined Meidum pyramid is the southernmost of the Old Kingdom pyramids that comprise the royal necropolis of Memphis. Nearly thirty miles up-river from the ancient capital, the pyramid stands alone, a gaunt and isolated tower rising starkly in two massive courses from the surrounding hill of rubble, left over from the collapse of the pyramid's surface layer. It may be, as one writer has suggested, that the Meidum pyramid collapsed only shortly after it was built.[1] Nonetheless, the attempt in itself was a gesture of assurance and daring in the technology of stone construction that was in keeping with the Fourth Dynasty's characteristic spirit of confidence and vitality. The culmination of that spirit would come in the following generation with the building of the magnificent Great Pyramid at Giza.

Merely to list the dimensions of King Cheops' Great Pyramid, as is so often done, can convey little of the awesome nature of the structure. Yet it seems worthwhile remembering that this massive man-made mountain of stone occupies a land area large enough to contain St Paul's in London and St Peter's in Rome – at the same time. It was built of locally quarried limestone from the Giza plateau, and then faced with fine

14

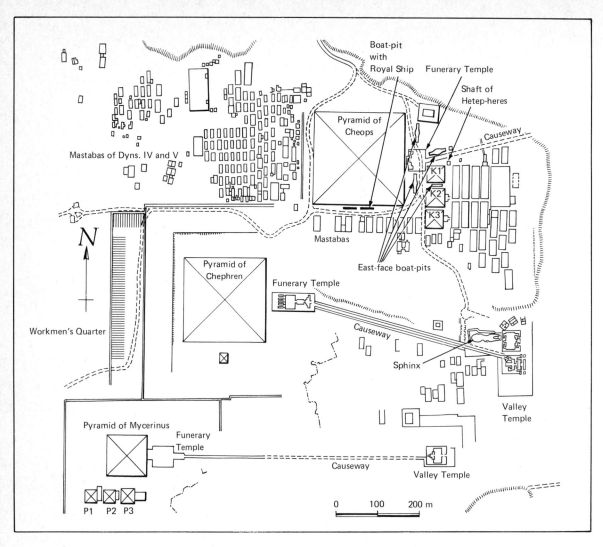

14 *The Giza necropolis, showing the boat-pits in relation to the Great Pyramid of Cheops. The secondary burial of Cheops' mother, Queen Hetep-heres, is indicated just behind the boat-pit adjacent to the causeway. Nearby are the three so-called 'queens' pyramids' (K1–3) and beyond them the mastaba graves of members of the royal family.*

white Tura limestone from the Muqattam hills behind modern Cairo. These facing stones were so precisely joined, the archaeologist Flinders Petrie pointed out, that not even a postcard could be inserted between them. The Mortuary Temple was dressed with pillars of red granite from Aswan in Upper Egypt; the black basalt paving stones of the temple courtyard can still be seen in place on the east side of the pyramid. When Herodotus described the roofed Causeway in the fifth century BC, it was still covered with relief carvings. Though these have long since disappeared, we can guess at their superb quality from the blocks and fragments of the Mortuary Temple that were re-used by a Twelfth Dynasty king in his pyramid at Lisht. Cheops' Valley Temple, at the foot 13 of the Causeway, has not yet been excavated, its ruins lying beneath the village of Kfar es-Sammân below the pyramid plateau.

Long before the discovery of the two sealed boat-pits on the south side of the pyramid, archaeologists had known of other open and empty pits 14 that had been excavated in the plateau close by the pyramid and situated in such a way that they were obviously part of the funerary complex. Two of these lie along the east face of the pyramid, just north and south of the Mortuary Temple. A third is aligned with the Causeway that leads 15 from the pyramid down to the valley. There is also apparently a boat-pit related to each of the three so-called 'queens' pyramids'. Unlike the more recently discovered sealed pits along the south face, which are both rectangular, these earlier known pits are all boat-shaped, narrowing and coming to a point at either end of the excavation in the rock. In addition to the pairs of boat-pits along the southern and eastern faces of the pyramid, there may well be similar pairs on the western and northern sides,

15 A view from the top of the Great Pyramid, looking down on the east-face boat-pits and mastaba tombs. The ruins of two of the three 'queens' pyramids' can be seen on either side of the smallest boat-pit. The dark ribbon of the modern road passes right over the foundations of the mortuary temple.

awaiting discovery by future archaeologists. Such a symmetrical arrangement would be in keeping with the pyramid's architecture. So far, however, nothing has been found.

Whether the boat-pits on the east face once contained real boats is not known for certain, though the American archaeologist George Reisner, who cleaned out one of these pits in the 1920s, certainly thought so. At the bottom of the pit he found bits of gilded wood and rope fibre, similar to what Emery subsequently found in the Saqqara boat-pits. Like Emery, Reisner believed this was solid evidence for a boat having once been buried in the pit.

16   One of the puzzles about the Fourth Dynasty is that there are more pyramids than there are kings to bury in them. The seven known pyramids are: the collapsed pyramid at Meidum; the Bent Pyramid and the Red or Northern Pyramid, both at Dahshur; the three Giza pyramids; and the ruined, possibly unfinished, pyramid at Abu Roash (Abu Rawwash). The six kings are: Sneferu; his son Cheops (Giza); Cheops' sons Djedefre (Abu Roash) and Chephren (Giza); Mycerinus (Giza); and Shepseskaf, apparently the last king of the Fourth Dynasty, who chose not to build a pyramid at all but went back to the simpler mastaba tomb.

It was once thought that the Meidum pyramid had quite clearly been built by King Sneferu, Cheops' father and the first king of the dynasty, a monarch much venerated in later generations for his legendary goodness. Some thousand years or more after the Meidum complex was built, an Eighteenth Dynasty scribe wrote on the walls of a temple there that he had come on a pilgrimage 'to see the beautiful temple of King Sneferu. He found it as though heaven were in it and the sun rising in it. Then he said: "May heaven rain with fresh myrrh, may it drip with incense upon the roof of the temple of King Sneferu." '2

But the late Ahmed Fakhry's investigations here at Meidum as well as around the Dahshur pyramids have produced evidence that Sneferu may not actually have built his own pyramid at Meidum, but completed one which his father-in-law and predecessor King Huni had begun. Later tradition mistakenly associated it with Sneferu alone. Kurt Mendelssohn has suggested in his book *The Riddle of the Pyramids* (1974) that, while Sneferu was in the process of erecting his Bent Pyramid at Dahshur, the Meidum pyramid suddenly and dramatically collapsed. Such a disaster might well account for the change in the angle of incline that gives the Bent Pyramid its characteristic and rather elegant rhomboid profile. Sneferu would have wanted to avoid, at all costs, the risk of his own pyramid collapsing as well.

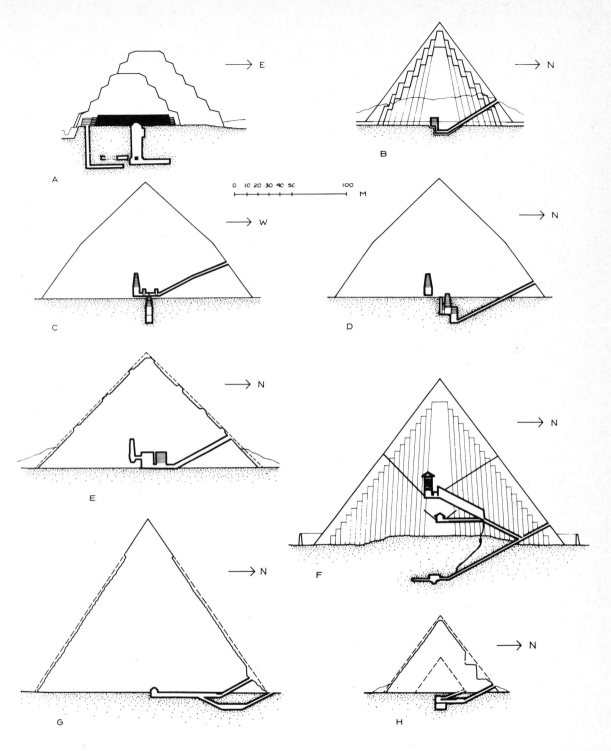

16 *The most important Old Kingdom pyramids shown in section with their entrances and burial chambers.* A, *the Step Pyramid of Zoser at Saqqara;* B, *the now-ruined pyramid of Meidum;* C, *the western, and* D, *the northern entrances to Sneferu's Bent Pyramid at Dahshur;* E, *the Red or Northern Pyramid of Sneferu at Dahshur;* F, *the Great Pyramid of Cheops at Giza;* G, *Chephren's pyramid at Giza;* H, *the pyramid of Mycerinus at Giza.*

17 *King Sneferu is shown clad in garments for the hebsed-ceremony and wearing the Double Crown of Upper and Lower Egypt on this five-metre-high stela. Set up outside the eastern face of the Bent Pyramid at Dahshur, the stela is taken to confirm that Sneferu did in fact build this pyramid himself.*

Egyptologists are certain that Sneferu had at least two pyramids. A legal document, dated some 350 years after Sneferu's reign, exempting 'the two pyramids of Sneferu' from taxes and the forced labour corvée, was found carved on a stone tablet near the Red Pyramid at Dahshur, evidence that this pyramid at least must have belonged to Sneferu. Fakhry's investigations at the Bent Pyramid, just south of the Red Pyramid, have shown that this monument too is without question Sneferu's. Among other evidence, a large stela found near the pyramid depicts King Sneferu clad in his robes for the *hebsed* rite, a magical rejuvenation ceremony that was celebrated periodically to re-invigorate the king's powers. Sneferu is shown wearing the two crowns, the bulbous white crown of Upper Egypt superimposed over the red crown of Lower Egypt.

It is not at all clear why Sneferu built two or more pyramids. Earlier kings seem often to have had at least two tombs, one at Abydos, the southern city that was sacred to Osiris, chthonic god of the underworld, and the other at Saqqara, within sight of the white-walled capital. Emery felt that the Saqqara tombs were the actual graves of the early kings, while the tombs at Abydos were cenotaphs, empty memorials for the King of

17

Upper Egypt. There would then have been another cenotaph for the King of Lower Egypt at Buto, another sacred city, in the Delta. Since most ancient structures in the Delta have long since disappeared in the silt of the annual Nile inundations, it is impossible to test Emery's hypothesis. Other kings besides Sneferu may have had two or more pyramids as well, or perhaps a pyramid and another, different sort of funerary monument, but if so we have yet to discover these other monuments – or to recognize them for what they are.

If the collapsed pyramid at Meidum is in fact attributable to Sneferu alone, together with the two Dahshur pyramids, then we are left with what one Egyptologist called 'the unpalatable conclusion' that Sneferu built three pyramids in the twenty-four years of his reign, an incredible expenditure of labour in so short a time. Herodotus was told that the Causeway *alone* of Cheops' Great Pyramid at Giza took ten years to complete, and the pyramid itself more like twenty. How then could Sneferu have managed so much in the relatively brief span of twenty-four years? Herodotus, who was after all writing more than two thousand years after the event, may have been mistaken. More recently Egyptologists such as I. E. S. Edwards have suggested, on the basis of blocks discovered at the Red Pyramid bearing quarry dates, that it may have taken considerably less than twenty years to construct these monuments. Nonetheless, anyone who has seen the vast structures, even in their present state, and can imagine the way they must once have looked, will wonder at the enormous expenditure of time and energy and labour and, above all, organization, they entailed.

The purpose and function of the pyramids has been a subject of debate, one imagines, almost from the time they were first erected. Somehow a mere grave, even for a personage as magnificent as the god-king of Egypt, seems an unimaginative use for such imposing structures. In the end, however, the evidence from nearly eighty pyramids (not all of them, by any means, from the time of the Old Kingdom) is overwhelming. The pyramid served two functions: as the repository of the dead king's remains it was a lofty monument to his memory; and, as the centre of the cult that was focused on the dead king, it was intended to secure his well-being in the afterlife for eternity – and thereby the eternal well-being of Egypt as well.

Funerary ritual

In his admirable book, *The Pyramids of Egypt*, I. E. S. Edwards has described the elaborate funerary ritual that took place when a king died. Edwards' description of this ritual is based on the Pyramid Texts, a com-

18 *A masterpiece of Old Kingdom sculpture, this diorite seated statue of Cheops' son Chephren probably formed part of a group of twenty-three similar statues in the Valley Temple to Chephren's pyramid. It was found in a deep pit in an antechamber to the temple where it had evidently been placed in ancient times in order to preserve it from destruction. Cf. ill. 122.*

(Opposite)

I The Great Pyramid at Giza seen in the evening light. The modern museum which houses the Royal Ship lies to the right in the photograph.

II The Giza pyramids at sunrise. The Great Pyramid is on the right, with the boat museum on its southern side. Cf. ill. 14.

plicated series of spells, charms and prayers found inscribed in hieroglyphs on the internal walls of the pyramids of the Fifth and Sixth Dynasty rulers, but dating originally from a much earlier period.★ The king's body would be brought to the Valley Temple from Memphis by boat, most likely in a papyriform funerary boat looking very much like the Royal Ship of King Cheops. The dead king's body was ritually bathed at the Valley Temple in an act of purification and regeneration of his spirit that recalled the Sun-god emerging regenerated each morning from the waters of the Lily Lake. It was the first step in a complicated yet precise ritual that guaranteed the revivification of the king and his survival in the hereafter. The most important ceremony was the 'Opening of the Mouth', a rite that was performed not on the king's body but on life-size statues

★ The earliest were found in the pyramid of King Unas, or Wenis, who was most probably the last king of the Fifth Dynasty, but in the main they are a Sixth Dynasty phenomenon. Internal epigraphic evidence, however, style, the use of language, the spelling of words, etc., suggest that they are often much older, and in some cases go far back into the predynastic period. Perhaps in earlier times they were written on more perishable material; certainly nothing has so far been found that predates King Unas.

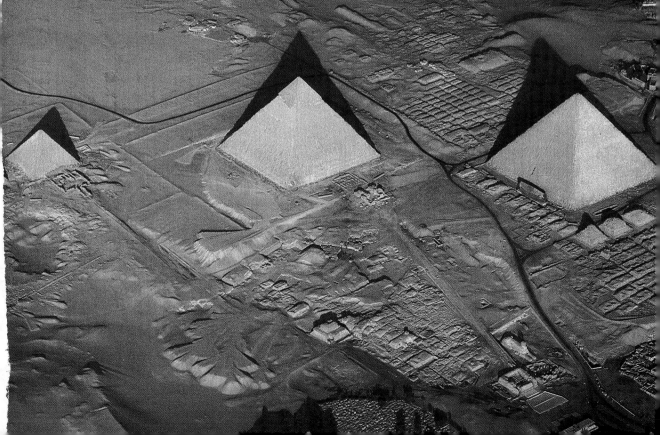

of him that lined the niches of the Valley Temple's central hall. (There were twenty-three statues, of diorite, schist and alabaster, in the central hall of Chephren's Valley Temple, the only Fourth Dynasty building of this type that remains relatively intact.) The king's son and successor would sprinkle water over each statue, cense it with aromatic fragrances, offer sacrifices before it, touch various sacred objects, including an adze and a chisel, to its mouth, then rub its mouth with milk and deck the statue in royal regalia. By this process each statue in the Valley Temple became animated with the king's divine *ka*, that part of his spirit for which 'soul' is a less than adequate translation.

18

Once these ceremonies in the Valley Temple were completed, the embalmed body, together with various crowns and the internal organs (which had been removed from the body to be embalmed and buried in a separate container) would be borne in a solemn procession in which only the ritually pure might participate, up the Causeway, the walls of which were sufficiently high to screen the sacred cortège from profane observation, to the Mortuary Temple where further 'Opening of the Mouth' rites were performed on statues of the dead king before his body was removed for its final interment within the pyramid. Whether the king's passing over to the eternal life was a joyous occasion or a time of deep mourning, we do not know, but it must have been a solemn event, charged with emotion and crackling with the potency of the magic that was being performed. No mistakes must be made, nothing omitted from the elaborate ceremony, for on the king's survival and well-being in the afterlife depended the survival and well-being of Egypt.

During the Fourth Dynasty, the king alone was entitled to this elaborate ritual, just as kings alone were buried in these great pyramid complexes. Even the king's first-born son, if he predeceased his father, was buried in a simple mastaba, as was the Crown Prince Kawab who died before his father King Cheops and was buried in a large mastaba just to the east of the Great Pyramid complex. We must assume that Prince Kawab's burial ceremonies, like those of other members of the noble classes, were equally simple.

Some Egyptologists have argued that the king was thought of as the mediator with the gods but not as a god himself. But during the Fourth Dynasty at least, the king does seem to have been considered divine. It was because he was thought of as the 'Great God' that the king alone partook of these funerary rituals and privileges. We shall go into the complicated subject of Egyptian religious beliefs later on, but it is worth stressing here how central this belief in the king's divine role was to the entire Egyptian system, whether theological, political or administrative, at least during the Old Kingdom.

(Opposite)

III One of the empty boat-pits on the eastern side of the Great Pyramid, looking southwest, with the pyramids of Chephren and Mycerinus in the distance.

IV The Royal Ship is today housed in a modern museum on the southern side of the Great Pyramid, built over the pit from which the ship was excavated. The limestone blocks covering the second – and as yet unexcavated – south-face boat-pit are just visible in the foreground.

Around the royal burials were organized the graves of officials, nobles, princes and princesses, to assist the king in death as they had done in his earthly existence. Outside the Great Pyramid complex, Cheops had erected a group of stone mastabas for his court. Sixty-four of these were laid out 14 in a regular pattern to form a little funerary village to the west of the pyramid. To the east were eight enormous twin mastabas for the king's favourite children, including that of the Crown Prince mentioned above. They were there both to serve the king in the afterlife and because their own survival in the afterlife depended on their proximity to the royal burial and the opportunity to share in its immortality.

No more convincing image can be given of the centralized absolutism of the Fourth Dynasty religious state than this association of the king and his servants for eternity. The state had been developed entirely to serve the god-king; he was the focus of all economic life as well as of all religion. Yet it makes little sense to speak of a personal authoritarianism, either of the king or of the priesthood, for the king himself, as much as anyone else, was prisoner and victim of the religious state.

Life in the Pyramid Age

The walls of the offering chapels in the mastaba tombs of the royal necropolis were decorated with carved and painted scenes from everyday life as well as inscriptions recounting the titles and achievements of the tomb owner. These offering chapels are one of our main sources of information about daily life in the Old Kingdom. Unfortunately little has survived from the Fourth Dynasty itself, but life during that century was probably not so very different from what went before or came after.

For the noble classes, it was a pleasurable existence. Agriculture was the main economic pursuit, though we hear of expeditions to the mines of Sinai and the eastern desert for copper and turquoise, to the mysterious land of Punt (Somalia? Yemen?) for exotic perfumes and spices, to Lebanon and Cilicia for cedar and other kinds of big timber that did not grow in Egypt. But it is the teeming life of the Nile Valley that is dwelt on most lovingly and in precise detail – ploughing and harvest, hunting 19 scenes in the desert and fishing in the great reed marshes that still lined the Nile banks, boating on the river in a variety of craft from simple reed rafts to great vessels oared and rigged for an ocean voyage, boat-building (here the detail has been invaluable, as we shall see, in understanding the construction of the Royal Ship), domestic pursuits such as weaving, making bread and beer. The flowering plants and the animals that populated marshland and desert, as well as the river fish, are noted with a closely

19 The hunting scene in the marshes, for thousands of years a favourite wall decoration in Egyptian tombs, is here represented by a relief carving from the mastaba of the Sixth Dynasty nobleman Mereruka, who was buried at Saqqara near the pyramid of his father-in-law, King Teti. Kingfishers, herons, flamingoes, ibis, ducks and other marsh fowl flutter in the reeds and perch on flower stalks. Four men punt a papyrus raft through the marshes while a fifth grasps the tail of a mongoose. In the water crocodiles and hippopotami battle with each other as fish swim calmly by.

observed naturalism and precision, and we can identify antelopes and hippopotamuses, papyrus, lotuses, ducks and other waterfowl.

These scenes of the rich life of the Nile Valley were favourites of artist and patron alike, for the patron had the security of knowing he would be surrounded, in the hereafter as in the present, by the same things that made life on the Nile banks such a deep source of pleasure, while the artist's talent rose to the challenge of depicting this life in all its variety. The charm and vigour of the chapel scenes is a tribute both to the artists' skill and to the deep love the ancient Egyptians felt for their cherished land. Altogether one has the impression, even if inevitably idealized, of a people leading active, energetic and productive lives, a self-confident people who lived in close harmony with their environment.

Of biographical detail there is very little from this period. Some centuries later, with the break-up of highly centralized royal authority, the nobles began to take sufficient pride in individual accomplishment to wish to record it for posterity, but from the Fourth Dynasty we have only

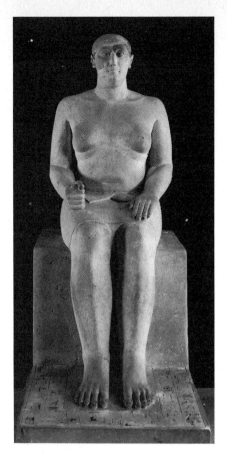

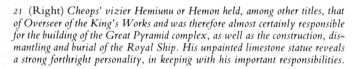

20 (Above) *This seated stone sculputure, almost certainly from the early Third Dynasty, is identified only as Bezmes, the ship-builder. He holds his boat-builder's adze in much the same way that the king holds the flail in royal sculpture.*

21 (Right) *Cheops' vizier Hemiunu or Hemon held, among other titles, that of Overseer of the King's Works and was therefore almost certainly responsible for the building of the Great Pyramid complex, as well as the construction, dismantling and burial of the Royal Ship. His unpainted limestone statue reveals a strong forthright personality, in keeping with his important responsibilities.*

titles. Sometimes these titles are tantalizingly descriptive, like that of
20 Bezmes, whose small statue is in the British Museum and of whom we know nothing more than that he was a boat-builder. Usually the titles are unenlightening honorifics, such as 'Great King's Companion' or 'Keeper of the Seal of Upper and Lower Egypt', that tell us nothing about the person or the office. Sometimes we can glean bits of information about relationships among members of the royal family. We know, for instance, that the Vizier Hemiunu, the 'Overseer of All the King's Works', was most likely the supervisor of the construction of Cheops' Great Pyramid, and probably of his boats as well. We can guess that he was a royal prince, a younger brother or half-brother of Cheops himself, because viziers, like other important ministers in the Old Kingdom, were usually close relatives of the king they served; and we gain an impression, from the life-
21 size seated statue of Hemiunu in the Pelizaeus Museum in Hildesheim, of a responsible leader and forceful administrator. There is something direct and honest about this man's large, handsome features, and it is pleasant to think that he may have been responsible for the intricate construction details of the Royal Ship.

If we know little of the biographical background or the personalities of the time, we know virtually nothing of the larger political and military events. One of the most important historical documents from the earlier dynasties is the Palermo Stone, a large diorite stela, so-called because the biggest fragment lies in a museum in the Sicilian capital city (there are other fragments in the Cairo Museum). Precisely engraved in long, regular columns on the black stone are lists of all the kings of Egypt, beginning with the near-mythical predynastic leaders about whom almost nothing is known, and continuing up to the kings of the Fifth Dynasty. Each year the height of the Nile flood was recorded, as well as any significant events that had occurred. Most of these events are records of temples built and offerings made, religious ceremonies and mining expeditions, but occasionally more dramatic episodes were noted down. Thus we learn that

22

22 The Palermo Stone lists the kings of Egypt from the mythical predynastic period up to the Fifth Dynasty. For each year the height of the annual Nile flood was recorded, as well as significant events, such as the building of a temple or the arrival of a shipment of precious wood from the Lebanon.

King Sneferu led a campaign against the Nubians in the south that netted 7,000 prisoners and 200,000 head of cattle, and another against the Libyans with almost equally significant results. But whether these were raids to protect trading parties, or expeditions for the express purpose of gathering slaves and cattle, or military campaigns of conquest, is not clear.

More directly relevant to the story of the Royal Ship is the information that Sneferu had sent an expedition most probably to Byblos, the important trading centre on the Lebanese coast north of Beirut. Forty ships returned to Egypt filled with cedar and other coniferous logs, and in the following years, it was noted, three ships, each some fifty metres long, as well as a number of barges, were built of wood from this shipment. Cedar was also used to make the doors of the royal palace, and it may have been part of this same shipment that was used for the beams in the burial chamber of Sneferu's Bent Pyramid at Dahshur – beams that can still be seen in situ by anyone agile enough to crawl through the narrow entrance passage.

Hetep-heres, Sneferu and Cheops

By fortuitous accident, and the meticulous attention of a skilled archaeologist, we know more about Queen Hetep-heres, Sneferu's wife and the mother of Cheops, than we do about any other Fourth Dynasty figure. In 1925, a photographer working in the Giza necropolis for the Harvard–Boston Expedition, literally stumbled over the secret secondary burial of this great queen. The excavation of the tomb, supervised by George Reisner, director of the Expedition, remains to this day a landmark, setting new standards for archaeology – careful, thorough-going, painstaking, above all patient – for, although the burial chamber measured only fifteen metres square, it took two years to sift its contents, so meticulous was Reisner's method.

23, 24 The contents of the grave were extraordinary – gilded furniture, chairs, a bed and canopy, a curtain box and coffers that contained the queen's delicate necklaces and bracelets. Elegant gold hieroglyphs proclaimed the owner of this fabulous equipment: 'Mother of the King of Upper and Lower Egypt, Follower of Horus, Guide of the Ruler, Favourite One, she whose every word is done for her, the Daughter of the God's Body, Hetep-heres.'

14 The grave was situated just south of the Causeway leading from the Great Pyramid to Cheops' Valley Temple, and just north of the three 'queens' pyramids'. It was the earliest intact royal burial yet found, but it was not complete. When the excavators lifted the lid of the alabaster sarcophagus, it was empty. The subsequent discovery in a wall niche of

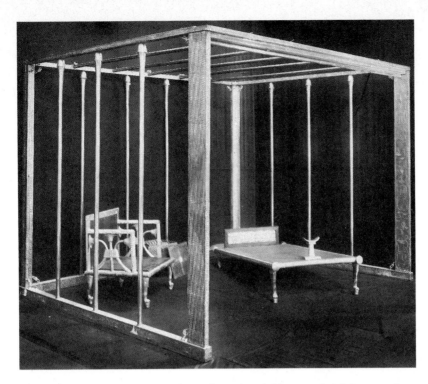

23, 24 The burial hoard of Queen Hetep-heres, the mother of Cheops, included this magnificent group of wooden furniture (above), sheathed in gold and decorated with the names and titles of the queen's husband, King Sneferu (right). The finials of the columns supporting the canopy have the same papyrus-bud shape as the columns of the cabin canopy on the Royal Ship (cf. ills. 34, 35), while the papyrus symbol is continued on the wonderfully simple openwork designs of the chair sides.

a smaller alabaster coffer, a canopic chest with the royal viscera still in their embalming fluid, could not compensate for the disappointment at the lack of a royal body as well.

In the normal course of things, Queen Hetep-heres should have been buried somewhere close by one of Sneferu's pyramids at Dahshur. Ahmed Fakhry believed that the Bent Pyramid, the southernmost of the two, was most probably Sneferu's actual burial place. It would seem that Hetep-heres' grave should be found nearby, perhaps in a small pyramid of her own. What then was the empty sarcophagus, accompanied by rich funerary equipment, doing in a secret burial at Giza?

Because she was called 'Mother of the King', we know that Hetep-heres must have died after her son Cheops came to the throne. Reisner's theory was that she had indeed been buried at Dahshur, but that thieves had broken into her tomb only shortly after she had been interred there, had prised open the sarcophagus and grabbed as many of the royal jewels as they could get away with, dragging her body out into the moonlit desert where, in their haste, they left it for jackals to consume. This rather

lurid speculation perhaps says something more about Reisner the novel-
ist than it does about Reisner the archaeologist, but if true it would have
been considered an appalling crime. The desecration of a grave was a terrible sacrilege, and especially the desecration of a royal grave. Indeed, the
disappearance of the queen's mummy, Reisner theorized, would have
been so horrifying that no one, not even the Vizier Hemiunu, would have
had the courage to inform the king of the crime. Instead King Cheops
would have been presented with the opportunity for a pious act, re-burying his mother's body next to his own final resting-place, still under construction on the Giza plateau, where she could share in all the prayers
and offerings that would be made to him. He would never have been
told that what he was re-burying was in fact an empty sarcophagus.

Hetep-heres was probably the daughter of Huni (or Hu), the obscure
last king of the Third Dynasty, about whom almost nothing is known
beyond his name. The title 'Daughter of the God's Body' was conferred
on the eldest daughters of reigning kings, and signified the important role
these women played in the succession. As far as the royal succession was
concerned, ancient Egyptian society was to a great degree matrilineal.
Women may not have been very important in society as a whole
(although one writer, Margaret Murray, has suggested that all property
descended in the female line from mother to daughter), but queens most
certainly were. The succession was guaranteed by the Daughter of the
God, the king's eldest surviving daughter and, properly, the daughter herself of a God's Daughter. This was the reason for the brother-sister mar-
riages of Egyptian royalty that are so troublesome to our minds: the only
way for a royal prince to secure his inheritance was to marry his full sister,
the Daughter of the God's Body. We can see the matrilineal roots of kingship also in the Palermo Stone, where each king's name is accompanied
by that of his mother, as a stamp of legitimacy and an accreditation of
his right to rule. An archaic hold-over from a more primitive era when
the father's role in conception was not clearly understood, royal matrilin-
eality continued to be important throughout Egyptian history.

Because of the dynastic change between King Huni, last king of the
Third Dynasty, and King Sneferu, first king of the Fourth Dynasty, it
seems probable that Sneferu was not Huni's son, or at least not his legitimate son by his principal wife. Sneferu must have gained the throne not
by inheritance but by marriage with the Royal Princess Hetep-heres, the
Daughter of the God's Body. They may have had many children. We
know of only one – Cheops – and him not very well.

Unfortunately, that part of the Palermo Stone dealing with Cheops'
twenty-three-year reign is completely missing, and there are no other contemporary documents that can contribute to our knowledge of his time.

The most ancient source we have is Herodotus, who visited the Giza pyramids some two thousands years later and claimed that the Egyptians of his day remembered Cheops, together with his son Chephren, as an impious and oppressive tyrant. Cheops, the priests at Heliopolis told Herodotus, closed all the temples in the country. 'Then, not content with excluding his subjects from the practice of their religion, he compelled them without exception to labour as slaves for his own advantage.... No crime was too great for Cheops.'

In fact, there is no historical justification for Herodotus' views; nor is there any evidence to support an opposite opinion. All that remains of the great king is the majestic pyramid complex at Giza and the magnificent Royal Ship that, together with an empty sarcophagus in the burial chamber of the Great Pyramid, is the only funerary equipment of his that we know. A little seated ivory figure, five centimetres tall, in the Cairo Museum is the sole portrait we have of the king. Found at Abydos in the temple of Khentiamentiu, the jackal-headed Lord of the Westerners, the figure is too small to give more than the most approximate impression of what the king really looked like. The expression on his face is of a rather wilful determination, but this may stem less from the portrait of the man than from Herodotus' description of him.

The pyramid-builders of the Fourth Dynasty represent the apogee of Egyptian civilization, the culmination of an extraordinary burst of creative energy that had taken place some five hundred years earlier when Menes united the Two Lands and traced the white walls of Memphis with his plough. From the marshy riverine beginnings in the reed shrines and simple pit-graves, from the first important stone structure, the Step Pyramid at Saqqara, from Meidum and Dahshur with their hesitant and tentative experimentation, to the Giza pyramids, and especially the Great Pyramid of Cheops, a sense of confidence grows, confidence in the material and the form, and in the power of the civilization to put them to use.

They were a people of enormous artistic skill and energy, intelligent and practical, organized around the principle that the state belonged to the divine king, that it existed to serve him and preserve him. Because of this assurance, they could tackle the problems of building a pyramid for a god's tomb in the same efficient spirit with which they approached the organization of irrigation and the securing of food supplies. Safe from invasion, either military or cultural, behind the natural boundaries of the Sinai and Libyan deserts, they were free to experiment with forms; yet deeply conservative and suspicious of anything that deviated from the fixed canons, they quickly settled on the pattern that was to inform Egyptian civilization for thousands of years to come.

25 *The Great Pyramid of King Cheops photographed from the southwest corner in the early 1930s, some twenty years before the discovery of the two boat-pits on the south face.*

CHAPTER THREE

Discovery

Exploratory work

Shortly after the Second World War, the Egyptian Antiquities Service, the official government body that oversees everything pertaining to the country's past, had drawn up a plan to clear away a century and more of rubble that had accumulated in the area around the Great Pyramid. It was a routine operation and there was no reason to expect any major discovery or even any new information, for the pyramids of Giza have been gaped at in curiosity and amazement since well before Herodotus wrote the first tourist guide some twenty-five centuries ago. King Cheops' pyramid particularly, with its immense scale and formal perfection, has always been a source of wonder and speculation. And since the Napoleonic invasion of Egypt in 1798, when eighteenth-century rationalism and systematic science were applied to the ancient civilization of the Nile, the Great Pyramid has been studied, measured, excavated, drawn, photographed and generally exploited, inside and out, by treasure-seekers, savants, archaeologists, astrologists, historians, mountain-climbers and hordes of the just plain curious. Everything that could be known about the Great Pyramid was known, it seemed, except for the still-puzzling question of how a society whose technology had not yet arrived at the wheel, was able to erect such a massive structure in the first place.

Throughout this century archaeologists excavating in the tombs of the Giza necropolis had used the pyramid area as a convenient dumping ground for their debris. Wind-blown sand from the desert had drifted over these dumps and formed great dunes piled so high against the sides of the Great Pyramid that from close up it was impossible to see the structure itself. All of this was to be cleared away, according to the plans of the Antiquities Service, but it could not be done carelessly or with bull-dozers, as one would clear a building site, for the piles of sand and rubble might well conceal artefacts or other information whose importance would not have been apparent to earlier excavators. In a sense, clearing

25
26

45

the debris was like clearing an archaeological site, for it was necessary painstakingly to scrape away the earth, level by level, in order not to miss anything. Even so, nothing of any special interest had turned up when, in the early spring of 1954, the workmen began to finish the job. Under the direction of a young architect-archaeologist named Kamal el-Mallakh, they were clearing the southern and final face of the pyramid where sand and debris had accumulated in a great pile some twenty metres high.

Like all the other Fourth Dynasty pyramids, the Great Pyramid had been erected on the limestone bedrock of the Libyan escarpment, the long, low desert mountains that border the Nile Valley to the west, at a spot where the ancient engineers had deemed the subsurface sufficiently strong to support the enormous, concentrated mass of the structure. In some areas around the Great Pyramid there was evidence of a paved courtyard that had been laid out on top of the bedrock and perhaps had surrounded the pyramid entirely. The modern workmen's instructions were to clear away the rubble right down to the bedrock, or to the paving-stones if they found them, which indeed they did – wide, well-dressed slabs of limestone more than half a metre thick, exactly like those that had been found in other places around the pyramid.

The discovery during this routine clearance of what appeared to be part of the southern section of the temenos or boundary wall that had once

26 *Section through the Great Pyramid, showing the mound of debris that covered the two south-face boat-pits before their discovery in 1954, and, in the inset, the pit that contained the Royal Ship, sealed by great limestone blocks with shutters.*

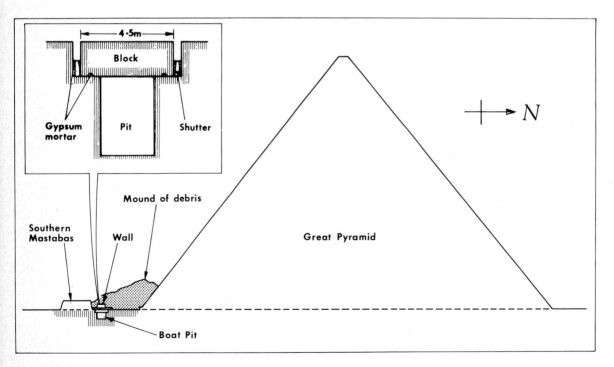

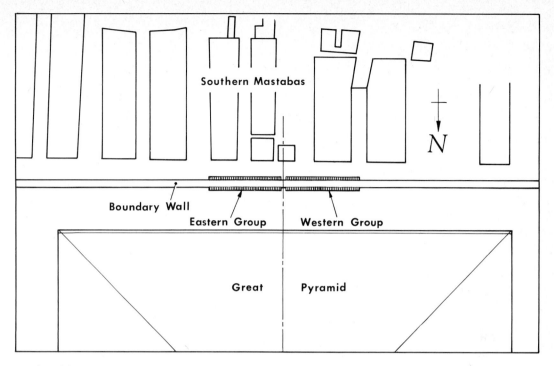

27 *Plan of the southern side of the Great Pyramid, indicating how the boundary wall overlay the forty-one stones that covered the eastern pit (with the Royal Ship) and the forty stones of the western pit.*

surrounded the pyramid complex was an unexpected bonus, but hardly surprising. Parts of the northern and western boundary walls were already known, and Herbert Junker, who had excavated the Sixth Dynasty tombs south of the Great Pyramid before the First World War, had mentioned the existence of a southern wall in his excavation reports – in fact, part 27 of the debris that covered the wall was rubble from Junker's excavations. Mallakh, who had studied the Swiss archaeologist's reports, had been hoping all along that Junker's wall, undestroyed, might turn up again beneath the mound.

In its original state this wall seems to have been nearly two metres high and to have extended from one end of the Mortuary Temple right around the pyramid on all four sides, connecting up with the temple again at its opposite end, and effectively sealing off the sacred precinct from contamination by anyone who was not ritually clean. The fairly solid base of the wall was constructed of limestone, granite and basalt chips, packed together in a sort of cement. These stone chips were probably the debris left over from the construction of the pyramid, the causeway which in its original state had had black basalt paving-stones, many of them still in place, and the Mortuary Temple with its columns of red Aswan granite. The boundary wall had then been smoothed over with mud-plaster and coated with a white gypsum finish, so as to look like the fine

28 Kamal el-Mallakh, now a Cairo newspaper editor, was in 1954 a young archaeologist, whose stubborn persistence led to the discovery of the Royal Ship.

white limestone that had sheathed the pyramid itself. In its rubble and plaster construction, the southern wall was exactly like the northern and western wall sections that were already known, and like them the outside surface of the wall had a slight batter or slope to it. What was different, and surprising, and a little disturbing to anyone sensitive to the ancient Egyptian's hankering for precision, was the fact that, although the northern and western walls were each precisely 23.6 metres from the base of the pyramid, the southern wall was a good 5 metres closer. Kamal el-Mallakh thought he knew the reason why.

29 The forty-one limestone blocks that sealed the pit with the Royal Ship. The dotted line represents the metre-wide shelf on which the blocks rested.

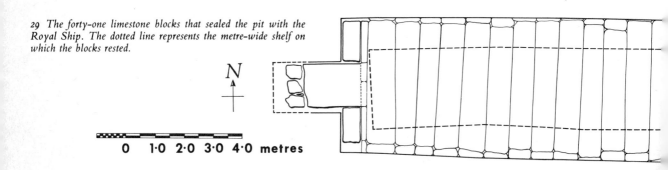

Mallakh is now Deputy Editor of *al-Ahram*, the respected, semi-official Cairo daily newspaper. He is a large man with a sparse fringe of iron-grey hair and a curiously quiet, soft-spoken manner that belies his importance in the cultural and intellectual life of the city – indeed of the whole country. Mallakh's first university degree was in architecture, and as an architect he had been assigned to the Antiquities Service in order to maintain the ratio between Egyptian and foreign employees in the department. Under the influence of the Abbé Drioton, the French priest who was then head of the Service, he had taken a second degree in Egyptology and become an impassioned student of his country's ancient history.

As soon as he realized that the southern section of the boundary wall was a good deal closer to the Great Pyramid than were either the northern or western sections, Mallakh became convinced that the wall had been built to conceal something. He had long been fascinated by the existence of boat-pits in connection with the Fourth Dynasty pyramids. There were five pits for boats (and possibly a sixth, unfinished one), carved in the bedrock outside the Mortuary Temple of the pyramid of Chephren just south of the Great Pyramid. Two of these pits are still partially covered with stone blocks, though no trace of a boat has ever been found. There is also an empty boat-pit just south of Djedefre's pyramid at Abu Roash, and another on the southeast corner of the curious Giza tomb of Queen Khentkawes, perhaps the last ruler of the Fourth Dynasty and almost certainly the mother of the first two kings of the Fifth. And of course there were the three empty boat-pits long known at the Great Pyramid, two outside the Mortuary Temple, and one aligned with the Causeway. Whether it is the operation of hindsight, or was an inspired guess at the time, Mallakh says now that he was convinced the south temenos wall had been built closer to the pyramid's base than were the northern and western walls precisely in order to conceal one or more additional boat-pits – solar boat-pits, as he continues to call them against the opposition of almost every other Egyptologist who has ventured an opinion on the subject.

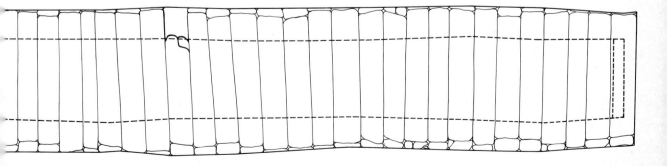

30 The name of Cheops' son Djedefre, enclosed in the cartouche that signified he was a king, was scrawled on many of the blocks that covered the pit – proof that Djedefre succeeded his father directly and not, as was previously thought, much later in the dynasty.

After exposing the southern wall by cleaning it of its surrounding debris, Mallakh's workmen found beneath it a layer of beaten or compressed earth, a mixture of rubble and ordinary mud, sun-dried to a hard plaster-like surface. This *dakkah*, as it is called in Arabic, stretched for some distance beyond the wall in both directions, north towards the base of the pyramid and south extending beneath the Sixth Dynasty mastabas that had been erected on that side of the pyramid, a proof that the beaten-earth layer had been laid down some time before the Sixth Dynasty tombs had been built. Mallakh had already ordered the workmen to clear away the *dakkah* in order to find out what lay beneath it, when, probing through the mud-plaster with a sharp stick, he found traces of the rosy pink mortar composed of calcium sulphate and iron oxide that was the characteristic hard cement used in the Old Kingdom. Completely by chance, Mallakh's digging-stick had struck the mortar between two of the monolithic limestone blocks that covered the boat-pit.

The boundary wall was parallel to the southern face of the pyramid, but the thin line of mortar, Mallakh quickly determined, was not: it extended right beneath the wall and came out on the other side. In his excitement, he urged the workmen on until that very same day they had cleared two of the massive limestone blocks, revealing, Mallakh recalled recently in his Cairo office, 'the huge and confident work of the Fourth Dynasty'. 'The ancient Egyptians', he explained, 'had been working in stone since the Step Pyramid of King Zoser in the Third Dynasty. Now, with the Fourth Dynasty, they were a hundred, maybe even a hundred and fifty, years later. They were quite, quite sure of themselves by then and it shows in the magnificent way they handled stone.'

One after the other, as the workmen cleared away the beaten-earth layer of *dakkah*, the immense blocks of limestone appeared, jutting out of the plateau like a set of crooked teeth or the broken keys of a very old piano. There were two sets of stones, forty to the west, forty-one to the east, apparently covering two separate pits, with a partition between the two pits that fell precisely along the axis of the south face of the pyramid. On one of the blocks, protruding slightly above the others that covered the eastern pit, Mallakh could read upside down part of the cartouche, the royal name enclosed in a sacred oval ring, of King Djedefre, third in the line of Fourth Dynasty kings, the son and heir of Cheops.

It was difficult, Mallakh recalls, to get anyone in the Antiquities Service to take his find seriously. Egypt was then in the throes of nationalist revolutionary change. King Farouk, who for all his faults had been a dedicated patron of Egyptology, had left and an obscure group of colonels, led by Gamal Abdul-Nasser, was in charge. Abbé Drioton had departed with the king and new men, Egyptians, were running the Antiquities Ser-

29

30

(Opposite)

V View aft along the port side of the reconstructed ship inside the museum.

vice. In this climate of political fervour, nobody had much time for ancient history. Mallakh was told that what he had uncovered was unimportant, part of the foundation of the pyramid, or perhaps more of the paving-stones of the courtyard. He himself was certain now, if he had not been before, that the blocks covered two boat-pits. But whether the pits were empty or actually contained boats, and, if they did contain boats, what condition the vessels would be in some forty-six centuries after their burial, were questions that could only be answered by opening the pits. And if they were in fact boats, even supposing they were in good condition, they might still crumble on exposure to the air, something that had actually occurred in a post-war Italian excavation when, in a matter of minutes after exposure, wall-paintings in Etruscan tombs had quite literally disappeared from the horrified excavator's view. Somewhat grudgingly, as Mallakh tells it, he was given permission by the Service to open a hole in the twenty-second block of the eastern group of stones.

Opening the pit

It was towards noon on 26 May 1954, near the end of the archaeological season, at a time of the year when the white desert light glares on the Giza plateau and the dense volumes of the pyramids seem to shimmer in the nearly intolerable heat. For days Mallakh's workmen had been chinking away at the great stone, slowly and with infinite caution, for there was no way of knowing precisely how deep the stone lay or what damage might be inflicted by a falling fragment on whatever was concealed beneath. When they had gone down two metres from the surface they arrived at a shelf or ledge, carved, as would later be discovered, into the two long sides of the boat-pit. On this ledge the limestone megaliths rested. It seemed clear that the excavators were only centimetres away from their goal and at this point Mallakh took over the hammer and chisel himself. When the last fragment had fallen away there was nothing to be seen but a dark hole in the stone, the darkness made even more impenetrable by contrast with the white glare of the sun outside. 'Like a cat', Mallakh recalls 'I closed my eyes. And then with my eyes closed, I smelt incense, a very holy, holy, holy smell. I smelt time ... I smelt centuries ... I smelt history. And then I was sure that the boat was there.'

Still unable to see anything inside the hole, he took his shaving mirror and reflected a beam of sunlight ('the beam of Re, the Sun-god,' he says) into the darkness of the boat-pit. With great good fortune, since here was proof that there was indeed a boat, the light fell precisely on the tip of a blade – one of a pair of rudders or steering oars that were more than six-and-a-half metres long and carved, shaft and blade alike, from a single

(Opposite)

VI The forward section of the ship on the port side.

53

piece of Lebanese cedar – lying where it had been placed four thousand and six hundred years earlier by the workmen of the Giza necropolis who had buried the ship.

The boat's discovery was an event of national significance. Mallakh was understandably elated. For weeks he had been, if not totally scoffed at, at least put down with the gently patronizing tones that seniors use for their promising but overly enthusiastic juniors. His first sight of the majestic steering oar had confirmed his hunch, and if further confirmation were needed, it came some days later when David Duncan, a photographer working for *Life* magazine, inserted a camera in the hole in the twenty-second block. The photograph, published in a lead story in the magazine, revealed at the far end of the pit the unmistakable shape of an ancient prow, carved in high relief to resemble a bundle of papyrus stalks bound with five strands of rope around the bowsprit. The bowsprit's form was familiar. It could be seen in hundreds of tomb reliefs and paintings as well as model boats, dating from the earliest predynastic times right up to the New Kingdom. It was a papyriform boat, a wooden boat built to look like the papyrus raft that was probably the most ancient Nile boat of all. Papyrus rafts were used throughout Egyptian history, for the most mundane purposes and for as long as papyrus reeds grew along the Nile, but even as early as the First Dynasty the reed raft seems to have assumed a special, possibly a sacred, significance, and its elegant shape was transformed and copied in the more permanent material, wood. Just as we can trace in the decorative and architectonic elements of Egyptian temples their origin in reed huts, so the ancestry of the wooden papyriform boat goes back to the impermanent and fragile papyrus raft.

1954 was an especially fruitful year for Egyptian archaeology. In that same month of May, Zakaria Ghoneim had announced his discovery of a hitherto unknown Third Dynasty Step Pyramid at Saqqara, buried in the sand dunes west of Zoser's pyramid. And Labib Habachi had found in the Karnak temple the historically important Stela of King Kamose from the early New Kingdom. Later that year Ghoneim and Mallakh were sent on a lecture tour of the United States, addressing learned academic audiences as well as making television and radio appearances. The trip was planned to inform Americans, scholars as well as the general public, of recent developments in Egyptian archaeology. It was also, Mallakh felt, a way of getting rid of Kamal el-Mallakh while plans were made for the boat's disposition.

Unfortunately an altogether unseemly quarrel had broken out almost immediately after the boat's discovery, a quarrel that still to this day has not been resolved even though many of the litigants died long ago. Twenty-five years later, the issues are as unclear as they were initially,

(Opposite)

31 An early photograph taken before the pit was completely uncovered, looking east towards the stern, reveals the remarkable state of preservation of the ancient ship's timbers.

but the substance of the argument seems to be the question of who should get credit for the boat's discovery.

As a general rule, archaeologists are publicity-shy, particularly at the moment of discovery. Long years of the most patient sifting of all the evidence, comparison with similar discoveries, weighing arguments and hypotheses, thinking, writing, reading, studying, conferring with other archaeologists and with historians, are required before any conclusions can be stated. Time and again, unwise archaeologists have been rushed by their own enthusiasm and that of the public into a sensational attribution that is later proven, if not totally mistaken, at least over-confident. But discoveries of the order of Tutankhamun's tomb or Cheops' Royal Ship are genuinely sensational and they generate their own publicity, inevitably distracting from the sober, scholarly atmosphere in which they should perhaps ideally be presented.

An unwarranted amount of publicity seemed to surround the discovery of the Royal Ship. The Duncan photographs appeared in magazines throughout Europe. Journalists clamoured for stories and interviews, and for several weeks news of the boat occupied the front page of the *New York Times*. Interest was high, both in Egypt, where Nasser himself set aside time to visit the extraordinary find, as well as in the world outside. Nonetheless, it was felt then, and is still felt by many today, that Mallakh had taken entirely too much of the credit for himself. Interestingly, the official Antiquities Department publication, *The Cheops Boats*, although it gives credit to others who worked on the boat at various stages, does not once mention Mallakh's name, and the whole tale of the discovery is told with an air of accidental serendipity that Mallakh himself categorically denies.

Despite the controversy, however, action was taken. The Antiquities Service had at last realized that the pit sheltered a unique and precious survival from the ancient world, and that in all likelihood the second pit contained a sister ship. A committee to oversee the excavation and restoration of both boats was quickly formed, drawing on all the expertise the Service could command. (At that stage of planning, it was assumed confidently that once the first boat had been rescued, the second could also be excavated; the western pit, however, remains unopened to this day.)

39 Included on the committee as a matter of course were Dr Zaki Iskander, head of the chemical laboratories of the Antiquities Service, and Hag
8 Ahmed Youssef Moustafa, chief of the restoration section. Both men would play vital roles in the eventual conservation and reconstruction of the ship.

The excavation of the Royal Ship was to be an entirely Egyptian undertaking, perhaps not the very first in the history of Egyptian archaeology, but one of the most delicate and certainly the most important. No conscious decision was ever taken to keep the project in Egyptian hands, but things being as they were in 1954, it seemed natural and normal that it should be so. The officers' revolt led by Gamal Abdul-Nasser was only two years old. In understanding the nationalistic fervour that swept Egypt then and that still to a large extent pervades Egyptian life today, one must remember that Nasser was the first Egyptian leader the country had had since the pharaohs of the Thirtieth Dynasty. Libyans, Nubians, Greeks, Romans, Arabs, Turks, and latterly the French and the British – for more than two thousand years the political life of Egypt had been dominated by foreigners, sometimes acting through native figureheads and puppets, but always in firm control.

Egyptology was born with colonialism when Napoleon invaded Egypt in 1798, and until well into this century, the study of ancient Egypt remained an exclusive preserve of foreigners, especially Europeans and Americans. One has only to read the roster of great Egyptologists – Lepsius, Maspero, Breasted, Reisner, Junker, Gardiner, Emery – to realize how thoroughly the field was dominated by westerners. Today, however, times have changed: the Antiquities Department is firmly in Egyptian hands, and a whole generation of Egyptian Egyptologists, men like Labib Habachi, and the late Selim Hassan and Ahmed Fakhry, to name just a few, has taken over. Such changes began it is true well before 1954, but the political events of the early 1950s in Egypt added an urgent impulse to the feeling that the study of ancient Egypt was properly a concern of modern Egyptians. It seemed right then that the excavation of the Royal Ship should be undertaken without recourse to foreign assistance, whether technological or financial. In a sense it would be a tribute to the new Egyptian patriotism.

CHAPTER FOUR

Excavation

Ahmed Youssef Moustafa

When he heard the news of the great discovery at the pyramids, Ahmed Youssef Moustafa was hard at work in the Eighteenth Dynasty tombs of the nobles at Thebes in Upper Egypt. The Theban necropolis stretches along the dusty, desert foothills of the Libyan escarpment on the west bank of the Nile, across the river's broad reach from the temple of Karnak and the somnolent modern tourist town of Luxor, once the site of Hundred-Gated Thebes, proud and glittering capital of the Egyptian Empire. For generations the west bank was the main burying ground of Thebes, a city of the dead to complement the city of the living on the opposite shore, and the foothills of the escarpment are honeycombed with graves.

Hag Ahmed had worked for twenty years in the Theban necropolis, recording and restoring the brilliant series of paintings that decorate the walls of these tombs. His colleagues in Cairo assure me that he knows every one of hundreds of graves there, by name as well as number. Often during the course of his work he became so involved that he would pass the night in the tomb, sleeping on the ground and dreaming that he was the tomb's owner – dreaming, he says, the dreams of the person who had been buried there.

As soon as he heard of the Royal Ship, Hag Ahmed downed his tools, a curious assortment of face creams and brushes that looks more like the contents of an actress's make-up box than the implements of a master restorer, crossed the river to Luxor, and took the overnight train to Cairo. It is difficult to imagine this patient and dignified old man in a hurry, but hurry is what he says he did, out to the Giza pyramids to examine the job he knew he would be called upon to do. Had he any doubts or misgivings when he peered through the hole in the twenty-second block and saw in the dim light the giant timbers, the stem and stern posts, of the Royal Ship? Did he realize the magnitude of the job that lay before him? 'At first,' he says, 'I was anxious and afraid. I knew nothing at all

(Opposite)

32 The topmost layer of the dismantled ship, from the eastern end of the pit, after the enormous limestone blocks had been removed. The oars can be clearly seen, and in the centre and background parts of what was later found to be the cabin assembly.

about boat-building, and it seemed that this job perhaps needed a ship-wright more than it did a restorer.' But then he realized that no one else knew anything about boat-building either. It had been more than half a century since the last discovery of this nature, the five or six small boats 100, 101 that had been found near a Twelfth Dynasty pyramid at Dahshur (see chapter six). There was no one left in the Antiquities Service who knew anything about the Dahshur boats, and the excavation reports were un-fortunately silent on exactly how they had been pieced together.

With his characteristic self-assurance Hag Ahmed realized that if the job could be done, then he alone would be the one to do it. And it had to be done. As he recounts the story twenty years later, there is a remark-able attitude of certainty about the whole thing, and it is difficult to re-member that it would be several years before he or anyone else knew precisely what was and was not in the pit.

In the late 1920s, when Ahmed Youssef Moustafa, still a teenager but with a first-class degree from Cairo's Institute for Applied Arts, had approached the Antiquities Service for a job, the art of restoration, at least as far as Egyptology was concerned, consisted largely in gluing back pieces of arms, legs and noses that had broken off stone sculptures. Anything made of less durable material than stone was of necessity ignored. Not only was the restoration technique primitive, but, like so much else in those days, it was entirely in the hands of Europeans. Egyptians, it was felt, especially young Egyptians like Ahmed Youssef, lacked the skills to work with such unique, often fragile, usually precious objects. For nearly four years, the young man worked in unhappy frustration, casting moulds and producing replicas of Cairo Museum pieces for other institutions around the world, and watching in anguish as the few attempts at restora-tion too often ended in a botched job that completely misinterpreted the piece. Over and over again, he asked for permission to try his hand at restoration, but his requests were ignored.

A single-minded obsession had governed his life since he was a small child, a belief in his unique gift, which is at heart a faith in his ability to understand and to communicate with the ancient Egyptian craftsmen and artists who first created these objects. The story is told of him that once, while working on a woman's head in a tomb in the Theban necrop-olis, he felt her flinch beneath the harsh scraper he was using. He switched to a wooden tool, but still the lines in her face spoke her protest. Only when he began to use a soft camel's hair brush, did she relax and a look of gratitude come over her features. This story is told in English while the old man, who speaks only Arabic, sits by with his hands folded placidly over his paunch and a benign smile lighting his face. One wonders if he believes the story. It is impossible to tell and is, in any case, not very important. What is important here is what the story illuminates about the nearly mystical sense this puritanical, orthodox and deeply religious Muslim has of being in touch with the pagan life of the ancient past.

'I made trouble at the department,' Hag Ahmed recalls in his deep, measured voice. 'I was patriotic. I wanted an Egyptian to restore Egyptian things, and I wanted to serve Egypt.' His perseverance and his unshakeable self-assurance must have impressed someone in the Antiquities Service in the end, for instead of being fired outright, as had been threatened, he was finally given a task to perform, an impossible task such as one reads about in fairy tales. He was given a shapeless chunk of mud-caked rubble with barely descernible bits of faience and plain and coloured ivory chips embedded in it. It was impossible to tell what sort of object, if any, might be concealed therein. Take as long as you want with it, R. F. Engelbach, then the museum's curator, told him, but don't come back until you've finished – implying, Hag Ahmed says now, that he expected never to see him again.

For weeks the young man worked at it. He made preliminary drawings. He cleaned the ivory chips and shifted them about in patterns. He made further drawings. Even in those early days his work was marked by a ruthless kind of patience and the indefatigable conviction that the answer eventually would come. Finally, when the month that he had promised himself had passed, he returned to Engelbach with what is now displayed in the Cairo Museum as the Akhenaten box, an elegant small ebony coffer, shaped like a miniature steamer trunk, inlaid with faience and an elaborate geometry of ivory panels.

In the desert rest-house where he lives, Hag Ahmed Youssef keeps a replica of the Akhenaten box which he willingly brings out for visitors who are curious about his work. Certain elements that he points to in the design were obvious to him, but others were utterly incomprehensible at first. It was like a jigsaw puzzle, he explains, using a metaphor that he will use again in describing his work on the Royal Ship, but a jigsaw puzzle without a picture on the box, indeed without a clue as to what the result was supposed to be.

The simple four-roomed bungalow where he entertains his visitors over glasses of lemonade and sweet mint tea is furnished with plain wooden divans and low tables, made by the Hag himself, and decorated with replicas and models, photographs and drawings of the precious pieces he has rescued, pieces for whose very existence he is often single-handedly responsible – a one-to-twenty scale model of the Royal Ship, photographs of the great boat at all stages of excavation and restoration, pictures of a Ramesside gold funerary mask, before and after reconstruction, a replica of a showy gold belt, studded with faience, (fake lapis) and tur-

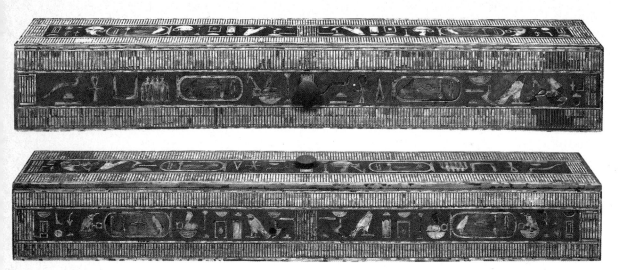

33 The curtain box of Queen Hetep-heres, meticulously restored by Ahmed Youssef Moustafa, formed part of the queen's burial hoard excavated by George Reisner in 1925. Top and side views show the faience inlay and delicate gold hieroglyphs set into ebony panels. Like those on the canopy whose curtains the box once contained, these hieroglyphs proclaim that the ensemble was a gift of Hetep-heres' husband, and Cheops' father, King Sneferu.

quoise, that once encircled the imposing bulk of some pharaonic official. Objects such as these are precious not only in terms of the monetary value, which is often considerable, but perhaps more so as works of art and carriers of information, witnesses from the remote and antique past.

Among the pictures on the walls of the rest-house are Hag Ahmed's drawings of the furniture from the burial hoard of Queen Hetep-heres that George Reisner had excavated in 1925 (see chapter two). Together with other members of Reisner's team, the Hag worked on the restoration of this extremely delicate and fragile material over a period of many years. Fragments of sheet gold, bits of faience inlay, and a fine ashy powder that had once been ebony and aromatic Lebanese cedarwood were all that remained of the queen's elegant furnishings. The reconstructions in the *23, 24* Cairo Museum, and the reproductions in the Boston Museum of Fine Arts, are a tribute to the skill and perspicacity of both the ancient craftsmen and the modern restorers. Hag Ahmed's particular pride is the long, *33* slender box with its intricate inlays of gold faience and precious woods that had contained the linen curtains of the queen's bed-canopy. The curtain box, together with the canopy itself, had been presented to the queen by her husband King Sneferu, according to inscriptions on the pieces. Much of the constructional detail and many of the decorative refinements in these pieces would be repeated in aspects of the Royal Ship. The joints of the bed-canopy were pegged and lashed together like those of the canopy that covered the ship's cabin, and the columns of both canopy and cabin had similar papyrus-bud and palmette finials, so that it is tempting to see them as products of the same skilled workshop connected with the royal necropolis.

34, 35

The severe grace of Hetep-heres' ensemble appealed to Ahmed Youssef's own pleasure in restraint and modesty. A man of simple taste, he has neither television, radio nor car and must rely on friends for transport between Cairo and Giza or anywhere else he might want to go. But what would be an agonizing frustration for a less patient person is yet another example of the Hag's unique composure. If a ride is not available immediately, *ma'alesh*, as the Egyptians say: never mind, there'll be a ride tomorrow, or the next day, God willing. The key to the man is in this sturdy conviction, perhaps grounded in his strictly orthodox religious belief, that the pattern of life is comprehensible. With this he combines the patience to wait for the pattern to reveal itself, and the intelligence to push the elements of the pattern in the direction in which they ought to go. 'He is a sheikh al-Azhar,' one of his Cairo acquaintances explained. 'It's difficult for non-Muslims to know what that means.' She was referring to the university that was founded in the tenth century in connection with the great Cairo mosque of al-Azhar. It provides the epitome of a Muslim religious education, something akin to the rigorous intellectual training of the Jesuits, which manages to expand the instrument of the mind at the same time as limiting the horizon of the mind's exploration.

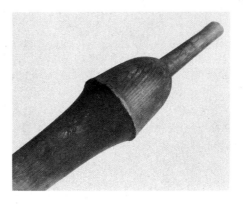

34, 35 *The papyrus-bud motif is at its most elegant in the finials of the gold-sheathed columns supporting Hetep-heres' bed canopy; but the same shape finished the columns of the cabin canopy on the Royal Ship – and it is quite possible that both canopies were products of the same palace workshop. Cf. colour ill. IX.*

The first stage

The Antiquities Service committee had taken the momentous decision to open the pit and to excavate and reconstruct the ship, although, it must be remembered, no one really knew for sure then whether the boat *could* be reconstructed, either wholly or in part. From the photographs that Duncan had taken, the wood appeared to be in a good state of preservation, but there was no way to be certain of its condition without removing the limestone blocks that covered the pit – and to remove the blocks without the most stringent precautions would certainly hasten the deterioration of the wood.

It was a dilemma that was resolved by the Chief Chemist, Dr Iskander. Priority, Iskander knew, had to be given to the preservation of the wood. Before any thought could be given to removing the limestone blocks and opening the pit, certainly before the boat's reconstruction, the actual condition of the wood had to be determined, as well as the question of how best to preserve it and to prevent any further deterioration.

Small and wiry, with thick dark spectacles that magnify his large eyes, Dr Iskander has a totally Egyptian sense of humour. He keeps a mummified duck in the drawer of his desk at Cairo American University where, in his retirement, he teaches classes in the chemistry of restoration. 'I did it myself in 1941,' he explains proudly, exhibiting the dark yellow carcass to visitors. 'You see,' he says, with an appreciative sniff, 'there's been absolutely no disintegration whatsoever.'

Dr Iskander had been a student, and then a colleague, and finally a successor of the late Anthony Lucas, whose great work *Ancient Egyptian Materials and Industries*, first compiled in the 1930s, is still the definitive study in the field. An exhaustive exploration of all the materials and methods of ancient Egyptian manufacturing, Lucas' book has very little in it about wood, particularly wood from the Old Kingdom. The reason is simple: wood is an organic material, far more fragile than ceramic or metal or stone, and even in the dry air of this desert climate, it is likely to deteriorate with time. Very little wood has been preserved from ancient times. There are a few wooden statues, such as the standing statue of the so-called 'Sheikh el-Beled', or the wooden panels from the Third Dynasty tomb of Hesy-Re at Saqqara, both pieces now in the Cairo Museum. But most Old Kingdom wooden pieces, such as Hetep-heres' furniture, simply disintegrated with time and what we see today in museums are modern reconstructions.

Dr Iskander had carefully removed a scrap of wood from the top of the pit and carried it himself to the British Museum's chemistry laboratories, where it was identified as cedar and was found to contain 10 per

36

36 The delightfully rotund figure of Ka-Aper suggested to his Egyptian excavators their own village headman, hence his familiar title of the 'Sheikh el-Beled'. The wooden sculpture is one of the few surviving examples of work in that medium from the Old Kingdom.

cent moisture, just a little under the average percentage (11–12 per cent) for ordinary seasoned timber in Egypt's exceptionally dry climate. A look at the hygrothermograph that Iskander had placed in the boat-pit showed the reason why. The pit had been sealed air-tight by a liquid gypsum plaster, imported from the Faiyum oasis and poured between and around the massive blocks of limestone, and it had remained that way for some four and a half millennia. Initially the wood, as well as the reed mats that had been laid on the surface, had given up a certain amount of moisture, but eventually an equilibrium had been reached. When the atmosphere within the pit had absorbed all the moisture that it could, it had become stabilized at a humidity level of 88 per cent. The temperature, at the same time, although susceptible to slight variations, hovered around a fairly constant 22°C.★ This accounts for the extraordinary state of preservation of the wood which, according to one witness, looked 'as fresh and new as if it had been placed there last year instead of almost five thousand years ago'.

★ These figures have been questioned by other laboratories in recent years. In particular, there is felt to be a discrepancy between the 88 per cent humidity in the pit and the free-water content of the wood (10–12 per cent). The suggestion has been made that the sample piece of cedar had dried out before it arrived at the British Museum laboratories. When and if the second boat-pit is ever opened, the figures that are obtained will provide a useful comparison with those from the first pit.

The balanced and stable environment in which the Royal Ship had been stored for all that time was about to be invaded. A shed had been erected over the entire boat-pit to house the big cranes that would be necessary to lift the limestone blocks. The largest of these enormous blocks was calculated by Salah Osman, the engineer in charge of removing them, to weigh just under sixteen tons. Dr Iskander counselled that each of the stones, as it was removed, should be replaced by a wooden block or beam, wrapped in fire- and water-proof cloth to protect the atmosphere in the pit. 'If we had left the pit completely open,' he explained, 'the water that had been sealed inside the wood for thousands and thousands of years would try to escape, and the wood would have been badly deformed or even destroyed. It was our job to keep that from happening.'

37 Using mechanical cranes and 'pickers', giant tweezers of steel that fitted over the ends of the blocks, it took just two months to remove the great stones. A crowd of journalists and dignitaries, diplomats, politicians and archaeologists, had gathered for the ceremonial removal of the keystones *38* and the first great block on 23 November 1954, just six months after Mallakh had peered through the hole in the twenty-second block. Once the first block was removed, however, there was not much to see, for Dr Iskander was insistent on his orders that each stone be immediately replaced with the wood block to preserve the atmosphere in the pit.

37 At the western end of the pit the keystones have been taken out and the great cranes manœuvred into place ready for the removal of the first of the forty-one limestone blocks covering the pit.

38 Removal of the first block on 23 November 1954, while a crowd of journalists, workmen and dignitaries looks on. Salah Osman, an engineer with the Department of Antiquities, supervised this phase of the operations.

Wooden wedges had been inserted between the first and second blocks to detach them from each other sufficiently for a lever to be manipulated between them. Since there was not enough room to use the 'pickers' on the first block, ropes were passed around it instead and the two cranes, balanced to operate simultaneously and keep the huge stone level, slowly lifted the first block clear. It was a tense moment. One slip, one mistake in calculations of stress, could have sent the massive rock crashing, but it rose slowly, ropes creaking from the great strain exerted on them, cleared the top of the pit, and was gently set down atop a series of wooden rollers. Workers then slid the great stone along the rollers to the outside of the shed. The cranes were the only modern touch. The wedges, ropes, levers and rollers were all devices that had been used by the ancient Egyptians, and had most probably been used by the workmen of Cheops and Djedefre when they moved these same stones into place forty-five centuries earlier.

At each end and along the bottom edge of every block were holes that seem to have been used to manoeuvre the blocks into place. Because the holes in the bottom were all along the western edges of the blocks, and because the keystones were at the westernmost edge of the pit, it was clear

39, 40 Dr Zaki Iskander, at the time Chief Chemist in the restoration section of the Antiquities Department, carefully applies a resinous solution to the fragments of ancient matting (seen in close-up opposite) *that covered the topmost timbers in the pit. This solution conserved the fragile vegetable fibres and made it possible to lift them without further damage.*

that the ancient labourers had worked from east to west placing the blocks. A rather large rectangular hole, cut into the bedrock of the plateau west of the boat-pit, probably had some function in positioning the blocks, but what similar circular holes some metres to the east of the pit had to do with the procedure is not clear to modern engineers.

But even if we could understand precisely how the stones were placed, it would still be a wonderful piece of work. We must remind ourselves yet again that these people in the third millennium BC had no wheels, no pulleys, no block-and-tackle mechanisms; yet they were able to quarry, cut and transport these monolithic sixteen-ton blocks, and to position them confidently over the pit's fragile contents, which would have been smashed to fragments had the slightest miscalculation caused a stone to slip.

Marks made by the ancient quarrymen are still visible on many of the stones, hieroglyphs scrawled in red and yellow ochre and in lampblack. They have the hasty and abbreviated look of foremen's instructions about how the stones were to be quarried. The marks apparently include references to measurements in cubits (the ancient Egyptian cubit was the equivalent of 52.3 cm), as well as the royal cartouche of Djedefre, the son of Cheops, the same cartouche that Mallakh had identified when he first uncovered the stones. With the exception of Djedefre's cartouche, which was already well known, the marks have not been identified. Further study may reveal more about ancient quarrying techniques. One thing the marks have established is the position of Djedefre in the Fourth Dynasty king-list: it seems certain that if he were the one to bury Cheops, he must logically have been Cheops' successor.

When the blocks were removed from the pit-head, the quarry-marks were all sprayed with a 7 per cent polyvinyl-acetate solution to preserve

30

them. Even so, time has affected them, and twenty-five years later the marks are almost illegible. The inscriptions on the huge stones that sit outside the boat museum are protected from sun, wind and dust by nothing more than that original thin spray and some boards laid casually against them to shade them from the worst of the sun.

The limestone blocks rested on the metre-wide ledge some two metres *29* down from the top of the pit. The blocks had been wedged into place with shutters, smaller pieces of limestone inserted at either end of each block to ensure a tight fit. It is impossible to think that the ancient builders were casual in their concern for the preservation of the boat, for every effort was made to seal the pit as tightly as possible. Were they aware of and concerned about the depredations of time, weather, insects? Or was it the knowledge of how the tomb of Hetep-heres, Cheops' own mother, had been so recently and ruthlessly desecrated that led them to make such efforts to seal and conceal?

On 28 January 1955, the final stone was taken out from the pit-head and it became possible, for the first time, to get an overall view of the pit with its contents. A composite photograph taken at the time showed *1* the topmost layer, covered with plaster dust and small chunks of gypsum

41 *The ship's prow, carved to represent the rope bindings of a papyrus reed raft, was found leaning against the western end of the pit. Expansion and contraction of the timbers had caused only slight damage, although the capping disc was split in two.*

that had fallen into the pit in ancient times. Beneath the dust was a layer of material, most probably linen, although it was far too disintegrated to identify it more precisely. The remains of cushion-like objects, layers of cloth that had been impregnated with resin, were perhaps fenders to protect the boat while docking. There were also ropes and mats that, although often extremely friable, fragmenting at the slightest touch, could be consolidated with resin and preserved. These mats and ropes were made of exactly the same materials as are used in Egypt today – at least where traditional materials have not been replaced by cheap plastics from China and Japan. Laboratory analysis later confirmed the original identifications that these were the commonest sorts of reeds and rushes, native to the Nile marshes since man first appeared on the banks of the great river.★ Dr Iskander has suggested that the word to describe certain types of these mats has remained almost unchanged from the ancient language of the hieroglyphs to the Arabic dialect that is spoken in Egypt today.

At the far western end of the pit, the columnar stem post representing a bound bundle of papyrus stalks had been easily and quickly identified from Duncan's earlier photograph. Now it could be seen more clearly, its two halves slightly askew and the disc that capped it split in two. The indentations were visible where rope lashings had once bound the sections of this prow together. Next to the prow piece two long curved and pointed timbers rose up from the bottom of the pit; they were matched by a counterpart pair of curved pieces at the opposite (eastern or stern) end of the pit next to the stern post, which itself again duplicated in wooden relief the tightly bound bundle of papyrus reeds that had been the first Egyptian means of water transport. It was already recognized that these curved and pointed pieces came together at bow and stern, and that the stern and stem posts most probably fitted over them in some manner. Towards the centre of the pit lay the long oar on which the sunlight reflected from Kamal el-Mallakh's shaving mirror had fallen. Disposed

31 over the surface was what appeared to be a confusion of smaller parts, including a series of joined wooden doors or decking, whose function was not at first apparent. Even then, however, at the initial sight of the whole ensemble, it was obvious that part of the solution to the puzzle that Ahmed Youssef faced would be found in the rational way the ancients had laid out their king's boat, not in a helter-skelter pile of timbers, but in an orderly fashion, bow to the west, stern to the east, port beams on the left-hand side of the pit, starboard beams on the right. Throughout

★ The mats were made of the culms of *phragmites communis* (common reed) and *juncus arabicus* (rush) and of the leaves of *typha australis*; the ropes were of the twisted leaves and culms of *desmostachya bipinnata* (Halfa grass).

the centuries and around the world boat people have been known for their tidiness, a necessary function of the cramped quarters in which most of them live. 'Shipshape' does not seem an inadequate description of the state of the pit's contents.

Hag Ahmed Youssef was not able to begin the exacting task of removing the wooden parts of the boat until December 1955, a year and a half after the discovery. Much had been accomplished in that time. Not only had the blocks been removed and set aside, but a proper restoration shed had also been constructed next to the shelter over the pit. Earlier in the year Iskander had supervised the consolidation and removal of the mats and cordage that were placed on the topmost layer of wood. Despite the friable condition of this material, Iskander was able to consolidate enough of it to include it in the museum display.

39, 40

42, 43 (Left) For the first stages of removal from the pit Hag Ahmed devised a platform that could be suspended by pulleys over the working area, thus enabling him to conduct operations without putting pressure on the elements of the boat itself. Here Hag Ahmed, on the left, is preparing to lift the cabin door whose sliding lock was shown in ill. 7. (Right) Midway down in the removal operation were revealed these long, slender, regularly notched timbers. It was immediately suggested that they were some sort of keel and that the boat's ribs would be found to fit into the notches – a suggestion that gave rise to much frustration during the course of reconstruction (see ill. 75).

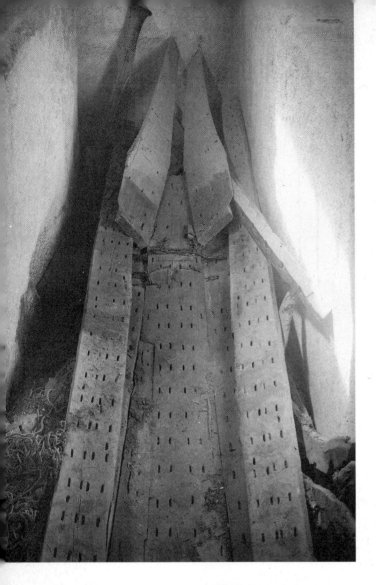

44, 45 *One of the lowest layers at the western end of the pit. The broad flat timbers of the ship's bottom clearly show the seam holes through which were threaded the ropes (below) that bound the vessel together. The papyriform prow (cf. ill. 41) can be seen next to the two curved blades on to which the prow would be socketed (cf. ill. 78).*

46 *At the eastern end of the pit the stern section of the bottom of the hull was discovered bound to the garboard strake on either side. Again, as in the bow, the two curved blades were intended to support the papyriform stern piece that raked back across the after deck.*

During this time Ahmed Youssef had not been idle. Although he had been an important member of the boat committee since it was first established, his primary responsibility would only begin when the pit had been opened and the uppermost surface of matting and cordage had been cleared, when, that is, the wooden parts of the great ship lay fully exposed. He had been working in restoration now for a quarter of a century, but, as we have seen, he had had no experience in restoring ancient boats, nor, in fact, any knowledge of the techniques of boat-building, whether ancient or modern. In this he was not alone. Twenty-five years ago, marine archaeology was something practised almost exclusively by treasure-seekers hunting for the gold of the Americas in Spanish wrecks. Of boat-building in pre-Roman times almost nothing was known. Today much of that has changed, largely through the work of marine

47, 48 (Left) The notched timbers shown in place in ill. 43 were in a fragile condition and difficult to remove owing to their length. A series of rope slings suspended from an iron bar, together with felt padding, solved the problem – although in this case still further reinforcement was needed from wooden boards. (Right) The same technique was used in the removal of the heavy beams that made up the bottom of the hull. On the pit wall, to the right in the picture, is one of the triangular reference marks shown in full in ill. 54.

archaeologists such as George Bass and Peter Throckmorton, who established a successful method of underwater excavation with the Cape Gelidonya wreck, of historians such as Lionel Casson and Björn Landström, who have consolidated information from many different cultures and historical periods, and of restorers such as Ahmed Youssef Moustafa himself, who, through a patient system of trial and error, became an expert on ancient Egyptian boats and the shipwright's craft.

In the beginning, however, Hag Ahmed knew nothing, and so, over the eighteen months after he had first examined the contents of the pit, he read and studied and prepared himself. There was not much to read, especially not in Arabic, the one language with which he was familiar, but there was a great deal to observe, in reliefs and paintings on the walls of tombs and in the hundreds of little wooden models of boats that became a requisite part of Egyptian tomb paraphernalia in somewhat later times. The biggest problem with all this material was that, although it was remarkably accurate as to finished detail, there was almost nothing about the process of construction. Only a few reliefs, such as Ti's Fifth Dynasty

tomb relief at Saqqara (see chapter six), showed boat-building in any   *102*
detail, and these details were easily open to misinterpretation. It is only
now, with the knowledge gained from Hag Ahmed's reconstruction of
the Royal Ship, that we are able to interpret accurately the constructional
details in Ti's boat-building relief.

Hag Ahmed pondered all of this material in his deliberate and methodical fashion. But, despite his learning, the Hag is a craftsman rather than a scholar, and like most fine craftsmen he is an intensely practical man. Much of his knowledge seems to come to him through his hands which, though large and square, almost crude looking, have a grace and fluency of expression, a gentle certainty of touch, that comes across in an act as simple as that of pouring a glass of mint tea for a visitor. In the end, he realized, the ancient boat timbers themselves would be his most valuable source material. The solution to the puzzle of the boat could only come about when he had confronted it himself, handled its parts in his own hands. Only then would he begin to understand their relationships.

In the meantime, he learned as much as he could about the construction of wooden ships. In the Nileside boatyards at Ma'adi, south of Cairo, and at Alexandria, Egypt's great port on the Mediterranean, he watched boatmen constructing everything from simple rowboats to the sleek Nile workboats that are such an elegant sight when their lateen sails swell before the north wind – or the big, bulky, square-ended *dahabiyehs* that carry travellers up and down the river. He watched, and he occasionally turned his own hand to the task, and as he gained confidence and understanding, he constructed by himself several big ten-to-one scale models, now in the museum, of the typical Nile boats. There was one enormous difference between the boats he was learning about and the boat that lay in the pit, but it would be some time before anyone realized this.

49 Dozens of metres of rope lay in coiled confusion at the bottom of the pit. By this stage it was clear that all this cordage was not, as had been originally surmised, rigging, but in fact the rope that had been used to hold the ship's timbers together.

Removal from the pit

By late June 1955 Dr Iskander had finished his work, consolidating and removing the uppermost layer of reed matting, but it was then too late in the season to continue. The intense heat of the Egyptian summer seared the desert plateau. Inside the pit the humidity was higher than that of the dry desert air outside and the temperature was much lower. It seemed wise therefore to keep the ship sealed in its pit throughout the long hot season that lasts well into what is called autumn in milder climates. Finally in December the wooden blocks were once more removed and the scaffolding devised by Hag Ahmed was set up to lift the pieces from the pit. This scaffolding was a simple affair, consisting of a wooden platform suspended just above the immediate work area in rope slings that could be raised and lowered, permitting work to proceed at close range without putting any weight on the timbers of the boat.

42

The responsibility faced by the Hag was overwhelming. Each piece had been laid in the pit with great care by the same people who had built

50–52 (Below) *At the very bottom of the pit each neatly tied bundle represented a separate assemblage of parts. Although it was not apparent exactly how the parts went together, it was obvious that they did somehow relate. (Above right) The broken sleeve of the prow, which after restoration would slide over the curved blades (ill. 78), cradled the most seriously damaged piece in the boat – one of the oars, reduced to tubular fragments by the weight of the timbers above. (Below right) After the main hull timbers had been removed, four of the limestone blocks that had supported them were revealed (near the centre of the picture).*

the ship and who thus understood the relation of its parts. Now those parts were to be removed by a man who had only a vague idea of what that relationship might be, and who moreover understood that a mistake at this stage might mean crucial information irretrievably lost.

A lesser person might well have been immobilized by the enormous responsibility of choosing the first piece for removal from the pit. The Hag's deliberate and practical approach seems to have concealed a certain hesitation even on his own part at the enormity of the task. Oars were easily recognizable, but what function the other parts might serve, what relationships their arrangement itself might hide, were at that stage imponderable. Indeed, the first piece to be removed and recorded in the registry book would give him quite some trouble later on. (That first *58–60* piece, as it turned out, was part of the little foredeck canopy.) But after this it was easier. Problems presented themselves – how to lift weak or *47, 48* cracked pieces, or the long beams that formed the great ship's side timbers, for instance – but they were problems that could be solved by that same deliberate practical approach.

There were thirteen layers in the pit. Each layer was photographed and the photos were squared metre by metre, so as to identify each segment with its contents in relation to the others. Then the individual pieces were photographed, drawn and given identifying numbers before being removed from the pit. In the restoration shed next to the pit each piece was described and recorded in the most meticulous detail, in both English and Arabic, then cleaned gently with an air-brush and treated with the solution of polyvinyl acetate for preservation. Under Dr Iskander's supervision the pieces were also treated when necessary with Markon resin in an acetate solution for conservation and consolidation, and with a 2 per cent DDT solution to lessen the danger of insect attack. Hag Ahmed had already recognized that the sections of the great ship were arranged in a logical sequence that would be part of the solution to the puzzle. That *61* sequence was maintained in the restoration shed. As each piece was removed, described and treated, it was placed in the shed in an order that followed, as much as possible, the order established in the pit.

Pieces that seemed similar in construction, or that appeared to have an analogous function, were drawn as they were found in the pit and the drawings were collated. This method was to prove especially useful with *32* the pieces of joined planking in the topmost layer. In the end, some of this was found to be decking, and some formed the sides and bulkheads of the deck cabin. Without the sketch of all these pieces together, months could have been wasted trying to fit together parts that did not belong.

It was without any doubt the most important excavation to have taken place in the Giza pyramid area since Reisner had uncovered Hetep-heres' secondary burial thirty years earlier, and in a sense it was Reisner's standards that governed the work. Dows Dunham, a member of Reisner's expedition and later Curator of Egyptian Art at the Museum of Fine Arts in Boston, described Reisner's method as essentially a process of dissection, taking apart and separating into its components a building or a group of remains or an object. In the very process of doing so, the evidence is of course largely destroyed. Only the most carefully detailed records, such, according to Reisner himself, as would enable future archaeologists and scholars to reconstruct the evidence precisely as it was found, could justify this destruction. In the Hetep-heres find, as in other less spectacular excavations, Reisner had set a model for future archaeologists to follow: square foot by square foot, each separate artefact, whether a recognizable object or an unidentifiable fragment, was photographed, drawn, measured and described, and its position in relation to other items noted.

The same standards prevailed in the excavation of the Royal Ship: the precise recording in minute detail, both on site and later in the restoration shed, the care in handling and conserving these fragile pieces, but above all the slow and thoughtful pace of the work that allowed time for

53 *The empty boat-pit, looking west. The wide shelf on either side of the pit supported the limestone blocks that had covered it.*

54 *These ten symbols, painted on the south wall of the boat-pit, have never been deciphered, but because of the crudeness with which they were drawn – evidence of hasty execution – it is assumed that they were workmen's instructions, either to the quarrymen or to those who were responsible for the ship's interment.*

mistakes to be corrected before they were irrevocable, were all part of Reisner's methodology. Although Hag Ahmed Youssef had never worked with Reisner on an excavation, he had, in a sense, absorbed Reisner's meticulous approach through his own work on the Hetep-heres furniture.

Hag Ahmed worked alone in the pit. Iskander and Zaki Nour, then Curator of the Pyramids Region, supervised the immediate tasks of identification, conservation and preservation in the restoration shed, but the job of removing the great ship from her grave was one that Ahmed Youssef chose to confront by himself. An overriding sense of his somewhat mystical connection with the past, particularly with the artisans and craftsmen of the past, whether stone-carvers, goldsmiths, potters or boatwrights, led him to his solitary occupation. Alone, without distractions, he felt closer to an understanding of what was contained in the pit. Holding each of the pieces in his own hands, hefting its weight, running his blunt, sensitive fingers over its contours, he felt he could find many answers.

In late June 1957, after two long seasons of excavation, the great limestone pit on the south side of the pyramid finally stood empty. Thirty-two-and-a-half metres long and five metres wide, the pit had contained 651 elements of the boat, such as cabin doors, walls, hatch covers and decking, which, when broken down into their component parts, amounted to 1,224 individual pieces (including all the major timbers). These were predominantly of cedar, although there were small details of acacia, sidder (*ziziphus spina-christi*), and other types of wood that grew natively in Egypt in ancient times as well as modern. The cedar had been identified at the British Museum as coming from that part of Syria that we know today as Lebanon, where the long and ruggedly graceful mountain ridges that separate the coastal strip from the interior were once carpeted with these massive evergreen trees.

With the exception of a few brads or staples of almost pure copper, there was no metal anywhere in the pit. The stones that had served to support the curving form of the hull pieces (and had perhaps been intended for ballast in the actual ship?) were removed during the course of the excavation, as well as metres and metres of rope, far more than

53

5, 7
52
49

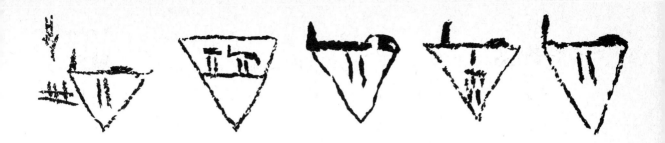

would have been thought necessary, interspersed between the layers and littering the floor of the pit. There was no treasure in the ship's grave besides the precious boat itself, not even a simple burial offering that might have revealed something more about who had buried it and why. There were no inscriptions except for the quarrymen's marks scrawled on the blocks and some strange, roughly drawn symbols enclosed in triangles (or inverted pyramids?) painted on the south wall of the pit itself.   54

Among the last pieces to be removed were a chunk of unworked black   55
basalt that might have been used as a hammering tool, and a narrow
flint implement, some fifteen centimetres long, precisely flaked in the
shape of a double-edged knife or chisel. These tools, together with a sherd
from a cheap, poorly baked, porous jug of the kind still used to keep water
cool through evaporation, were the only extraneous or, in archaeological
terms, foreign objects found on the site, carelessly dropped or knocked
into the pit by the ancient workmen. One can imagine the curses of the
knife's owner as he perhaps watched his precious flint fall irretrievably
down through the layers to the bottom of the pit – silent curses, no doubt,
for he was in a sacred place and the grave of the god-king was only a
few cubits away.

55 Three 'foreign' objects were found in the pit – a flint blade, presumably a workman's knife; an un-worked chunk of black basalt, perhaps a hammer-ing tool; and a sherd of cheap, common pottery, possibly a fragment from a broken water jug.

56 Ahmed Youssef Moustafa with a small model of the hull of the Royal Ship. The forward part of the hull is in the foreground and it becomes clear how the curved blades join together to form a prow over which the papyriform sleeve fitted (cf. ill. 78).

CHAPTER FIVE

Construction and reconstruction

'It is the duty of the restorer, before touching his patient, to make himself absolutely sure of the success of his operation so that no further loss of material or damage may happen to the valuable treasure in his charge. After long study and painful trials I came to the conclusion that the only way to assure success was to retrace the steps of the ancient maker and do again what he did long ago in moulding his masterpiece....'

Ahmed Youssef Moustafa, 1947

Piecing together the puzzle

Inside the brick-walled restoration shed next to the empty boat-pit, the warm and dusty air was fragrant with the resinous perfume of ancient cedar. Peace and tranquillity had returned to the desert graveyard high on the Giza plateau. The lifting cranes were silent, the workmen had mostly gone, tourists were few and more interested in the massive hulks of the pyramids than in the work going on in the shed, the journalists had long since departed, their excitement over the initial discovery replaced with the boredom that sets in when a task is long, tedious, complex and uncertain of result.

He had personally selected the few assistants who would help him with the job, but Hag Ahmed was alone with the responsibility. In the solitude and stillness, the enormity of the task revealed itself. At last he could appreciate the prodigious size of the ship, as well as the effort that would be required of himself to put it all back together. The 1,224 pieces of the puzzle ranged in size from pegs a few centimetres long to the two huge twenty-three-metre timbers that would eventually form the central sections of the sheer or top strakes on either side of the ship.

But his confidence, Hag Ahmed says now, never once faltered. Remarkably, his highly justified faith in himself was never shaken. He was certain that the puzzle could be solved, and equally sure that its solution lay there in the restoration shed, in the timbers of the ship itself. This was not mysticism, he assured me in talking of this time later on, but a deeply pragmatic approach: there would be only one way ultimately to put the ancient ship together, and eventually he would find that way, though it might, in fact did, take him years to do so. The visitor who is fortunate enough to see the boat in its museum today is struck by the extraordinary rightness of the reconstruction. This feeling of inevitability, this impression of a rational and well-planned system in the boat's construction, is a tribute both to the ancient shipwrights and to Hag Ahmed's perspicacity, but it conceals the effort, the months and years of trial-and-error before the Hag was certain that he had the reconstruction right.

Hag Ahmed's work on the Royal Ship has revealed so much about the construction of ancient boats that one tends to forget that when he began almost nothing was known for certain. Despite the hundreds of different boats depicted in reliefs, paintings and models, very little was understood about the all-important internal construction of ancient ships. Almost the only evidence came from the boats that had been found at Dahshur by the French archaeologist Jacques de Morgan in 1893, which were believed by their excavator to have been part of the burial equipment of the Twelfth Dynasty king Sesostris III, near whose pyramid they were discovered. Although they were ill conceived and appear to have been hastily executed, nonetheless they gave some valuable clues about boat construction. Another clue came from Herodotus' statement that 'the

100, 101

57 *A view from the south face of the pyramid in 1963, looking down on the restoration shed and, immediately beyond it, the empty boat-pit. To the right of the pit, the remains of the temenos wall can be seen with the blocks covering the second boat-pit jutting out beneath it. Today the restoration shed has been dismantled and the glass-walled museum covers the empty pit. (Cf. colour ill. IV).*

58–60 *The little baldachin on the foredeck of the Royal Ship was one of the first pieces to be reconstructed (below, left and right). A valuable clue came from the baldachin on the foredeck of Sahure's Ship of State depicted in a Fifth Dynasty relief fragment (right). The relief clearly shows the bow of a papyriform boat very similar to the Royal Ship. Ill. 59 shows the individual parts, the two curved struts that held the roof pieces in place and the columns with papyrus-bud finials like those on Queen Hetep-heres' bed canopy (ills. 34, 35).*

[Egyptian] boats have no ribs', although this was usually dismissed as yet another piece of misinformation provided by the 'father of history', also known as the 'father of lies'.

Hag Ahmed's work method, though it might appear aimless and haphazard to anyone unfamiliar with the problem, was in fact the only way to proceed. There were never fewer than four or five projects going on in the reconstruction workshop at any one time. Some of these were abandoned when they proved to lead nowhere; some obviously brought immediate results; most were projects that would be taken up and dropped, tinkered with and then put aside for a while, set to simmer as it were on the back of the stove. Painstaking notes and records, complete with

diagrams and photographs, had to be kept of every aspect of the reconstruction, whether it eventually proved successful or not. There were parts of the puzzle that suggested a prompt solution, such as the little baldachin on the foredeck, so similar to the one pictured on the bow of Sahure's
58–60 Ship of State (p. 134), or the canopy over the cabin, so like the canopy
23, 93 over Queen Hetep-heres' bed furnishings that Hag Ahmed had helped to restore twenty-five years earlier. Other pieces presented problems so complex and unfamiliar that it is a wonder the Hag did not give in to feelings of despair.

Two sets of clues had revealed themselves early on. As we have seen, it had been clear even while excavating the pit that the ship's parts had not been arranged casually or haphazardly. Precisely what the meaning of the arrangement might be was not something that could be immediately understood, but Hag Ahmed had wisely decided not just to record the arrangement of the pieces in the pit, but to preserve it as much as

61 In the restoration shed the parts of the Royal Ship were laid out as much as possible in the order followed by the ancient workmen when they buried the ship. Here, two sections of the floor beams have been temporarily pegged together, with the bow section in the foreground; the starboard timbers are stacked on the left and the port timbers on the right in the picture.

possible in the restoration shed. It was as though the pit had expanded *61*
in all directions without disturbing any of its layers, merely spreading
them out over a greater surface. Long before the pit had been emptied
completely, the logic of the arrangement had become obvious: as we have
seen previously, the prow of the ship was at the western end of the pit
and the stern to the east; starboard timbers were along the north side,
on the right as one faced the prow; port timbers on the south or left-
hand side. The various elements of the superstructure were in the topmost *32*
layers of the pit, while the hull pieces lay at the bottom and around the *44–46*
others, cradling them just as the hull had cradled the contents of the fully
constructed ship. Of course, the rigours of time and decay had caused
some shifting and settling of the contents, so that not all the parts were
where they had been placed by the ancient workmen, but in general it
was possible to follow this scheme throughout.

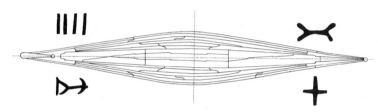

*62 Four general classifying signs were used to indicate forward, port and starboard,
and aft, port and starboard, quarters of the ship. Most of the timbers were marked
with one of these signs to indicate where they belonged.*

Another clue to the eventual reconstruction lay in the fact that many
of the wooden pieces of the ship had been marked with hieratic signs to
denote to which section of the ship they belonged. (Hieratic was a more *62*
rapid system of writing that had developed very early from hieroglyphs.
As a kind of shorthand, it bears much the same relationship to hieroglyphs
as modern cursive penmanship bears to the letters of a mechanical printing
press.) ✚ stands for the forward right-hand section, or quarter, of the
boat; ✕ for the forward left-hand side; ⤳ for the starboard after
section; and ⅠⅠⅠⅠ for the left-hand side in the rear. The German Egyptologist Wolfgang Helck, who has studied the signs most recently, has
shown that they represent broad general classifying words that refer not
just to ships but to almost anything constructed or under construction.
The parts of a tomb, for instance, are sometimes described with these signs,
and they can even be used at times directionally, with the sense of left
and right, or east and west.

63 In addition to the four general classifying signs (ill. 62), many other carpenter's marks helped in position-ing pieces. The marks shown here indicated where battens should be placed over seams between the hull timbers.

As well as these four general classifying signs, there were dozens of other marks left on the wood by the ancient carpenters, some of which are illus-

63 trated here. These marks have not yet been adequately studied or inter-preted, but they are obviously also directions of a sort, although more specific than the four general classifiers. Although they could not be given a precise meaning, they were nonetheless invaluable clues to the position-ing of certain pieces in relation to others.

Restoration and research

Before reconstruction could begin, the restoration work had to be com-pleted. The wood had been preserved in Dr Iskander's solution of poly-vinyl acetate immediately upon removal from the pit, but that solution merely inhibited further decay; it did not rectify decay that had already set in. In some cases the decay was considerable, particularly of pieces that had been placed or had fallen near the bottom of the pit with the weight of tons of cedar lying on top of them. If these were to stand up under

the stress of reconstruction, they would have to be strengthened. Sometimes a patch of wood over a weak spot was all that was needed. At other   *70, 71*
times new wood was built up around a core of old wood, or alternatively,   *64–67*
if the core was weak, strengthening members would be inserted while   *68, 69*
preserving the external appearance of the beam. Some parts had to be
replaced entirely with new wood, but there were surprisingly few of
these, for the wood as it was removed from the pit was in astonishingly
good condition. Throughout the exercise, the idea was not to disguise
the new wood so that it looked old, nor conversely to spruce up the old
wood like new. Rather it was to strengthen the old wood wherever necessary in a manner that would be both true to the original and at the same
time apparent to future archaeologists so that there could be no possible
confusion between work of the Old Kingdom and its modern imitation.

All the while there was the pressure of time, not weighing on Hag
Ahmed Youssef and his workers, but on the Antiquities Department
which was understandably anxious to produce results, dramatic results
that would justify the long wait. The boat had been discovered during
the spring of 1954 and uncovered with all the attendant publicity. It was
the late autumn of 1957 before Hag Ahmed was able to begin work on
its reconstruction and there were important people who had grown im-
patient in the meantime.

It is difficult for western Europeans to understand the depth of nationalistic sentiment in countries such as Egypt, where a remote but glorious
past and the memory of a once mighty empire are combined with more
recent experiences of the humiliation of colonialism and the bitterness of
a nation's impotence to shape its own history. Pride and shame are mixed
to a bewildering degree, and there is the additional pressure of the con-
sciousness, rightly or wrongly, that foreigners, with their money and the
expertise and technology at their command, could perhaps do a better
job, and could most certainly do it faster. It had become a matter of
national pride that the reconstruction of the Royal Ship should be finished
soon.

But in the end it was the patient, slow, sometimes apparently plodding
method of the traditional craftsman that would bring the most satisfactory
results. Hag Ahmed refused to be hurried without good reason. All that
first year he had his assistants engaged in making one-to-ten scale drawings
and models of every single piece that had been found. In this way he hoped
to be able to experiment freely without subjecting the old timbers to too
much stress. Meanwhile, he himself was still studying modern boat-building whenever and wherever he could. It was the basic structural principle
that he was after. Boat-builders, we have already noted, are extraordinarily
conservative by nature, and their basic principles have remained much

RESTORING THE ANCIENT
TIMBERS

64–67 *Before the ship could be reconstructed
restoration work had to be carried out. This
timber, part of a sheer strake, had been found in
relatively good condition except for the scarfed
end in the foreground which shows some
deterioration. The pictures illustrate the process
by which new wood was built up, encasing and
strengthening the old, and enabling the strake to
withstand the stress of incorporation in the reconstructed ship.*

68, 69 Some of the hull timbers were badly damaged. In this case a strengthening beam is inserted inside the old timber. The old wood is, as it were, peeled away from its decaying core. The new core is inserted within a framework of laths that provide for a tight join between new and old wood.

70, 71 (Below) The central shelf or stringer that formed the spine of the ship was badly cracked (see ill. 47, showing removal of this piece from the pit), and it required a patch of new wood.

the same throughout the millennia that men and women have been putting to sea. There remained a fundamental difference, however, between boats as they were constructed in modern Egyptian boatyards and the boat Hag Ahmed was trying to reconstruct. It is a difference that we have touched on before.

Basically, there are two ways of building a wooden boat, inside-out or outside-in. Most modern European and North American wooden boats are built inside-out, beginning with the skeleton, the keel and ribs, on to which the skin, or outside surface of the boat, is attached. Contemporary Egyptian boat-builders operate within this tradition. An older and more universal tradition is to build outside-in, that is, to build a shell of planks that are joined edge to edge, into which a strengthening framework is then inserted. In frame-built ships, the hull planking is joined to the ribs or frames; in shell-built ships the hull planks are joined to each other and are structurally independent of any framework. All ancient Mediterranean boats that we know of, right down to the Byzantine period, were edge-joined shell constructions, and it is a tradition that is still strong in

72 The bottom, or central, plank, was made up of eight timbers in three sections, forward, midships and aft. Laying out the timbers was fairly easy, but the difficulty came in determining how the three sections were related, particularly what their angles of abutment should be. On this depended the vital question of the bottom curvature, or fore-and-aft rocker, of the ship. Notice how much greater is the curvature at this stage than it was in ill. 61.

73 *The same care was taken at all stages of the reconstruction. During a trial assembly, one of the garboard strakes on the starboard side is moved into place. At each point of contact the ancient wood is protected by blankets and rolls of heavy industrial felt. To avoid undue stress the whole timber is supported by a steel I-beam.*

India and Asia. Some time in the Middle Ages, however – and no one is at all certain when – the Mediterranean tradition changed from shell-built to frame-built ships. It seems likely that Egyptian ship-building changed at the same time, or that the change possibly took place a little later, when Portuguese merchantmen rounded the African continent and entered the Indian Ocean, permanently affecting the construction of large cargo vessels in that area. Nonetheless, the tradition that produced the Royal Ship, as well as the Dahshur boats and probably every other ancient Egyptian wooden boat too, was the shell-built, edge-joined tradition.

Without question the most important element in a boat's construction is the shape or profile of the hull, which is in turn determined by the rocker, the curvature of the keel or bottom planking of the ship, and the sheer, the curve of the upper edge of the hull. The profile is the first thing drawn by the naval architect, whether he is building an admiral's flagship or a fishing punt for his own use, for on the profile depends everything else that has to do with the eventual boat, her shape, her size, her strength, and the way she will stand up to the job for which she is built.

74 *Looking aft, a trial assembly of the hull, curiously high and narrow compared with the shape of the final ship.*

Right from the start, then, there was a serious problem in rebuilding the Royal Ship, for because of her peculiar construction, it was impossible to tell what the curvature of the keel planking had been originally. Hag Ahmed had quickly determined the shape the keel planking should take, an elongated ellipse much broader amidships than at either end, as well as the way in which the eight separate timbers that made up the ship's flat bottom should fit together. The peculiarity of the Royal Ship, however, is that this keel planking has been constructed in three separate sections – forward, midships, and stern or after section – as a glance at the

81   strakes drawing will confirm. The midships section had been found lying on the floor of the boat-pit, and the forward and after sections were on top of it, overlapping the midships section front and back, which is how a forty-three-metre-long ship could be fitted into a pit that was only thirty-two-and-a-half metres in length. It was not difficult to work out that these forward and after sections should be joined to the midships section, so that the whole bottom, laid out flat, looked as it does in the strakes

94

75 *Another trial assembly that was to prove mistaken. Note that the long, slender, notched timber (see ill. 43) is lying in the bottom of the ship, since it was still felt at this point that it functioned rather like a keel into which the frames or ribs would fit. Only later did it transpire that this 'stringer' was in fact a central shelf which ran the length of the ship and supported the thwarts or deck beams, giving the structure its necessary rigidity (cf. ill. 80).*

drawing. But the biggest problem remained; at what angles should the butted ends of these sections fit together, the after section to the midships, and the midships to the forward section, because on these two angles would depend the curvature and profile of the ship? And there was no indication of how to solve this problem except through trial and error, putting the pieces together over and over again until they looked and felt right, and worked together with the other parts of the ship. (I realize that talking about the curvature of a flat-bottomed ship may present some problems to those who are unfamiliar with naval architecture. The curvature refers to a line drawn from bow to stern down the middle of the boat's bottom, where the keel would be if she had a keel. A line drawn across the ship, from port to starboard, at any point on the boat's bottom, would be straight, because her bottom is flat.)

61, 72

By the end of the first year, Hag Ahmed and his dozen assistants had produced three hundred scale drawings and ninety model pieces – out of the total of more than twelve hundred pieces of the ship itself. 'Clearly it was going to take us a good ten years to do the job. And I was quite prepared to take that,' Hag Ahmed recalls. But if ten years was a mere drop in time's bucket for the Hag, impatience in the Antiquities Department was growing acute. At the end of 1958, a new department head suddenly and unaccountably announced to the press that the 'Solar Boat' would be finished in three months' time. Rather than denounce this rash and intemperate statement, Hag Ahmed set himself to meet the impossible goal. He still would not be rushed – indeed, in the end, the task took longer than the ten years he had predicted – but now, he says, having spent most of the previous year with the Nile boat-builders and under their direction made the large models that are displayed in the museum, he felt confident of his ability to work directly on the original timbers of the Royal Ship.

The reconstruction

There would be a number of false starts and dead ends before the boat's profile was determined, but once that decision was finally reached, it was possible to make template pattern forms, what modern boat-builders call 'moulds', to control the curvature of the hull. It seems unlikely that the ancient Egyptian shipwrights used moulds – certainly there is no suggestion of them in any of the many tomb scenes that show boat-building – but they were enormously useful in the reconstruction, especially because they helped to relieve the strain on the old timbers. Once they had served their function of establishing the pattern of the hull curve, they were removed and they form no part of the completed boat.

One of the most interesting problems presented by the construction of the Royal Ship was the manner in which the carved papyriform stem and stern pieces were attached to the boat. In Viking and other North European ships, the separate stem and stern pieces, often themselves of great elegance and grace, are scarfed on to the ship's keel, but the Royal Ship had no keel, and the papyriform stem and stern were socketed on to the actual hull timbers. Hag Ahmed had postulated this from the very first when he spied the twin pairs of long, blunt-ended blades, shaped like lance heads, at either end of the pit, next to what were instantly recognized as the stem and stern posts. The position of the blades suggested to him that they were in some manner the connection between the decorative papyriform pieces and the main body of the boat. It was an inspired guess and a brilliant piece of intuition, for in fact the two pieces slid on to the blades like gauntlets sliding over a sleeve. The high stem post rising from the bow, and the stern post raked back over the afterdeck, are enormously heavy, but the ingenious manner in which they have been socketed on

76, 77

44, 46

78, 79

76, 77 Once the silhouette and section profile of the boat were understood it was possible to make template moulds around which the skin of hull timbers was erected. When the hull structure was complete, the moulds, having served their function, were removed.

prevents them from breaking off at bow and stern, and in fact contributes to the overall strength of the structure. Curiously, if the carved papyriform pieces are removed from the boat, one is left with an ordinary river travelling boat with truncated ends, such as the one being built in the lower register of Ti's great boat-building scene (see chapter six). Is it possible that this is not an ordinary boat at all, but that Ti's workmen are engaged in preparing a papyriform funerary boat, perhaps for Ti's own mummy? An alternative suggestion is that, at least by the time of Ti in the Fifth Dynasty, special funerary boats were no longer built; rather, papyriform fittings were grafted on to ordinary river boats whenever they were needed.

102

Now the great ship was coming to life once more, the timbers of her hull strakes bound edge to edge, sewn together with a simple but effective over-and-under stitch that holds the strakes in place while allowing a certain resiliency and mobility under pressure. There are an incalculable

80

78, 79 One of the most interesting aspects of the ship's construction is the way in which the papyriform bow and stern pieces fit like sleeves over the fore and aft sections of the hull. In the final assembly in the museum (below), we can see how the bowsprit slides over the bow, to produce the magnificent papyriform shape of the completed ship (opposite).

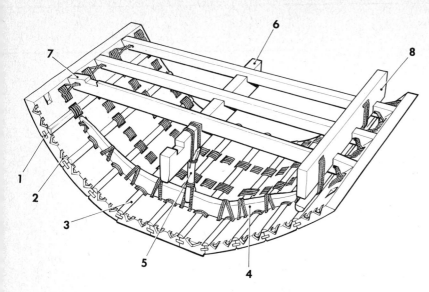

80 *The internal structure of the Royal Ship: the hull planks are held together partly by pegs (1), but more importantly by a system of ropes stitched through seam holes (2) that do not penetrate to the outside surface of the boat. Long, thin, hemispherical battens (3) are lashed over each secm, making caulking unnecessary. Frames (4) inserted into the hull to strengthen it support a series of stanchions (5), which in turn carry the weight of the central shelf or stringer (6) that runs the length of the ship. The thwarts or deck beams (7) are let into the notches of the stringer. Side shelves (8) similar to the central stringer rest on the thwarts and give further rigidity to the hull structure.*

number of forces that a ship must be able to take at any given moment, from wind, waves, currents, the strains of the ship's own movement, the weight of cargo. A properly built hull will accommodate all these forces, yielding and resisting in a harmonious balance. The Royal Ship, though she has never been floated in modern times, seems to have just such a hull, far stronger than what would be required for a ceremonial funeral barge.

Viewed from the outside, the ship's hull presents a smooth, streamlined skin. None of the lashing or stitching can be seen, for the V-shaped binding holes do not pierce through the cedar planks which are thirteen to fourteen centimetres thick. As in the work of a first-class tailor, the stitching is

83 hidden in the interior. Only where the stem and stern pieces actually lash on to the ship's ends was it necessary to bring the lashing outside, and

82 at these points, curved rectangular pieces have been bound over the knots to conceal them. Because of the inevitable warping of the huge timbers,

132 it is possible today to see some of the stitches in the gaps between strakes, but when the ship was new, from the outside one would have had no idea how she was held together.

Inside, she is an initially confusing jumble that assumes a rational order

81 only on close inspection. The garboard or bottom strakes, next to the keel planking, and the sheer or topmost strakes, are each made up of three timbers; the binding strakes have two; and between the garboard and binding strakes on either side of the ship are three extra planks, stealers, inserted to fill out the swell of the hull; there are thus eleven planks on each side of the hull. One rope can be threaded through the whole transverse girth of the ship, securing all the planks together. The planks are joined at their ends by S-shaped hook scarves, and their edges are also hooked to give a close, firm fit. In shipwrights' terminology, the planks are set 'carvel', that is, edge to edge, rather than lapstrake, with the edges

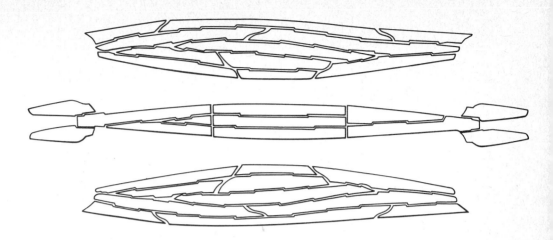

81–83 (Above) *A drawing of the strakes of the Royal Ship (bow to the right) shows the relationship of the hull timbers and the way they have been hooked and scarfed together. (Left) Curved rectangular battens conceal the ropes lashing the papyriform stern piece to the stern section of the boat. Similar battens serve the same function in the bow. (Below) The interior of the completed hull, showing the over-and-under stitching that binds the timbers together (cf. ill. 80). Modern steel braces help to support the deck hatches overhead. Some carpenter's marks can be seen in the left foreground.*

80 overlapping. In addition to the lashing that binds them, the planks are pegged together with mortise-and-tenon joints at various points along their edges. On the inside of the hull, long, thin battens, hemispherical in section, are lashed over the seams between the planks to make caulking unnecessary. And at either end of the ship, the two pairs of lance-shaped blades mentioned above are bound and pegged to both the bottom and the side planking, and the papyriform stem and stern pieces slide over these.

Sixteen frames or floor beams, big curved pieces shaped from a single piece of cedar, are inserted into the hull and lashed to the hull planks to strengthen it. On the frames rest a series of seven forked stanchions which support, in their turn, the long stringer or central shelf that runs down the middle of the ship. This stringer adds a longitudinal stiffening to complement the lateral strengthening that is provided by the thwarts or crossbeams, forty-six of which are let into the stringer at regular notched intervals. The ends of the thwarts are let into notches in the sheer strakes on either side of the ship. One of these thwarts, just forward of midships, is broader and thicker than the others, and Björn Landström has suggested that it is intended as a support for a two-legged mast, although no such mast, or any other evidence of sailing gear, was found in the pit.

84 Erecting the cabin on the still incomplete ship in the restoration shed.

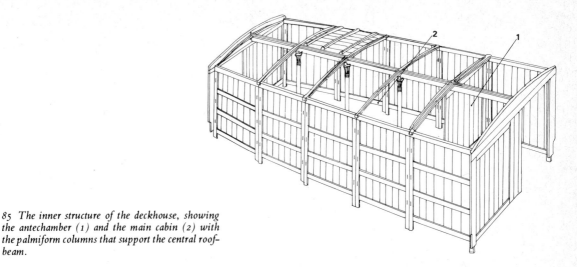

85 The inner structure of the deckhouse, showing the antechamber (1) and the main cabin (2) with the palmiform columns that support the central roof-beam.

A long side-shelf or girder runs down each side of the ship, resting on the thwarts. Between these two girders the decking is laid over the thwarts in a series of removable hatches. On the foredeck, ten slender poles, their finials carved, like those of the main deck canopy, in the elegantly re-strained form of a papyrus bud, support the small baldachin or canopy. It is not certain what this canopy is intended to shelter from the sun: an image of the god? a lookout? the captain or first mate or other important ship's personnel? perhaps a priest in charge of a ceremonial journey?

The main deck cabin, situated just aft of midships and extending between the side girders from one side of the boat to the other, is built up of twelve wooden screens or panels, five on each side and one at either end. A double door with a sliding bolt to lock it from the inside leads from the foredeck to a small antechamber, and another similar door connects this antechamber with the main cabin space. Within the cabin three columns with palmette finials, like those on the carrying chair of Queen Hetep-heres, support the central roof beam. A single door leads from the cabin back to the afterdeck. The door from the foredeck and the door into the main cabin are positioned in such a way that the oarsmen, standing (or seated?) on the foredeck, would be unable to see into the main cabin. The interior of the cabin on a hot summer's day on the Nile must have been a dark, humid and airless space Apart from the doors, there are no openings, and no passage for a cool breath of air to pass through. However, according to Hag Ahmed Youssef, there was a way, an imaginative way, to cool the cabin, for the whole structure is surrounded by thirty-six columns, again with papyrus-bud finials, that support slender beams arching some fifteen centimetres over the roof of the cabin. Hag Ahmed

84

59, 60, VII

85

7

90

89

93, IX

86 Part of a cabin wall panel indicates the care exercised by ancient craftsmen in carving patches to fit holes left by knots in the cedar.

87 The cabin wall panels were found as complete pieces in the pit. They were taken apart and rejoined, both to check on the condition of the wood and to understand their construction.

88 (Below) Assembling the cabin in the museum with Ahmed Youssef Moustafa (lower right) looking on.

89 (Above) *Looking forward from the cabin antechamber to the foredeck with the sliding door lock (ill. 7) in the centre foreground.*

90 *Interior of the main cabin looking towards the antechamber.*

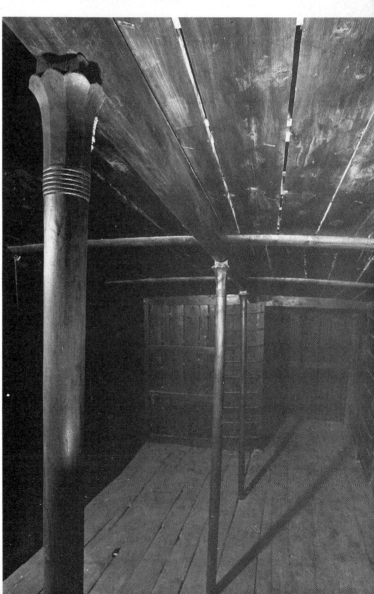

believes that this open framework was intended to support a layer of fabric, probably reed mats woven in brightly coloured geometric patterns like those that are often depicted on boats in later wall-paintings. If this matting were kept wet constantly with buckets of river water poured over it, it would provide a primitive but highly effective kind of air conditioning, a space of water-cooled air acting as an insulator around the roof and sides of the cabin. The canopy extends several metres beyond the cabin on to the foredeck to provide a shelter for the oarsmen from the searing summer sun.

There are five pairs of oars, varying in length from about six-and-a-half to nearly eight-and-a-half metres, on the foredeck, and an additional pair of steering oars, each a little over six-and-a-half metres long, off the afterdeck. Whether these actually provided the boat's propulsion is debatable. Lionel Casson, who has studied ancient Mediterranean boats extensively, believes that a ship of this type may have been towed by another boat, and that the oars and steering oars served simply to keep her on course. It is entirely possible, as we shall see, that the oars were not manned

79, 92, 93
134

91 *View aft along the starboard side, with the little gang-plank leading off the forward deck.*

92 (Right) *Two of the ten oars, five to a side, that provided at least part of the ship's forward momentum (the ship may have been towed as well as rowed). Note the arrow carved on the blade of the oar in the foreground.*

by seamen at all, but by people who had a more ceremonial or ritual function.

All in all, Hag Ahmed was to put this great ship together five times before she reached her final resting place in the museum next to the Great Pyramid. The first complete reconstruction was achieved by 1968, ten years after work had started on the actual timbers. Because of problems in locating the museum site, the boat was in fact taken apart and reassembled several more times. Hag Ahmed is confident now that the final, fifth reconstruction is the most satisfactory. In the end, he had reduced his reassembly time from nearly two years to about three months, so familiar had he grown with the elements of his puzzle.

93   The completed ship is 43.4 metres long and 5.9 metres in the beam. Her depth, measured vertically from the base line to the level of the upper deck planking at the position, just aft of midships, of maximum width, is 1.78 metres. Her maximum draught is 1.48 metres at this point of maximum beam and her displacement is about 45 tons. In the water, her hull timbers would expand and the rope lashings shrink to make a strong, flexible, watertight vessel. A ship whose planks are stitched together seems strange at first, but in fact it was until recently the characteristic way of building sea-going vessels in the Arabian Gulf and in port towns and shipbuilding centres all around the Indian Ocean. Today the tradition is dying

93 A composite photograph shows the completed Royal Ship as she stands in the museum today. The bow is to the left, facing west, as it was found in the pit.

out, though apparently a few examples can still be found in places like Dhofar, but at one time sewn boats were used in the extensive China trade when Arab ships sailed from the Gulf as far as Canton, Foochow and other South China ports. Lionel Casson points to evidence that Classical writers knew of sewn boats as an earlier, more primitive, tradition in the Mediterranean. Virgil describes Aeneas crossing the Styx in a 'sewn skiff'.

Sewn boats have not been known in Egypt in modern times. Whether the tradition was typical of all ancient Egyptian boat-building, or whether it was something reserved for vessels as spectacular and as special as the Royal Ship, whether it was a continuing tradition or whether it was alive only during the Old Kingdom, are questions that cannot presently be answered. As with many great discoveries, the Royal Ship asks as many questions as it answers, opening up new and often unsuspected areas of inquiry that must await further discoveries before they too can be resolved. At the same time, the Royal Ship, in its construction as well as its reconstruction, has told us much that we did not previously know about ships and ship-building in ancient Egypt.

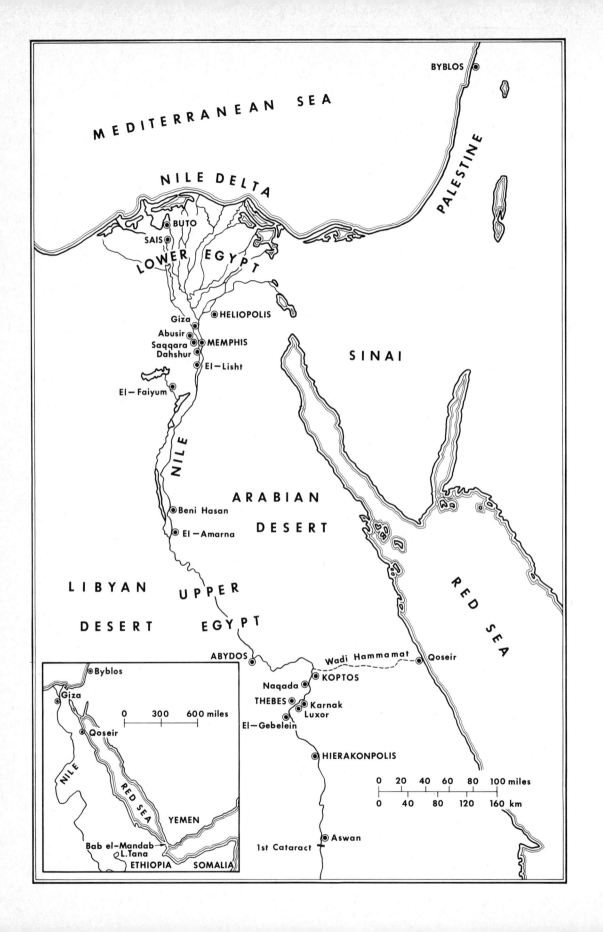

CHAPTER SIX

Ships and ship-building in the Old Kingdom

> I went down to the sea in a boat one hundred and twenty cubits long and forty cubits wide. One hundred and twenty sailors from among the best of Egypt were in it. Whether they looked at the sky or whether they looked at the land, their hearts were fiercer than those of lions. They could tell a storm wind before it came and a downpour before it happened....[1]

From Byblos to the land of Punt

Thus begins the tale told by the shipwrecked sailor, an oriental fantasy worthy of Sinbad himself, a fable of storm and wreck and miraculous rescue by a gold-plated basilisk with lapis-lazuli eyebrows. By the time the 'Story of the Ship-Wrecked Sailor' was first written down, probably during the Eleventh Dynasty, early in the second millennium BC, the Egyptians had been a seafaring nation for at least a thousand years, travelling north across the Mediterranean to Syria and the Cilician coast and southward down the Red Sea towards the Horn of Africa and beyond.

From the town of Coptos on the Nile just north of Luxor, they would cross the eastern desert, taking the well-travelled but nonetheless perilous route, eight days' march through the valley of the Wadi Hammamat where many of them left their names or other inscriptions on the cliff walls, to the port town of Qoseir on the Red Sea coast. Here at Qoseir the actual sea voyage began, some 1,300 miles down the Red Sea to the land of Punt, the semi-fabulous country that lay somewhere beyond the Bab el-Mandab, in Somalia or the Yemen, and that provided the Egyptians throughout their history with gold and frankincense, leopard skins, ivory and ebony. It has long been a matter of scholarly dispute whether the ancients trekked entire boats across the mountainous desert from the Nile to the Red Sea, or whether they transported to Qoseir the actual timber from which the boats would be built. Certainly nowhere on the inhospitable Red Sea shores was there a supply of timber sufficient to build sea-going trading vessels. The sophisticated construction of the Royal

94

(Opposite)

94 *Old Kingdom Egypt was a political and cultural unit from the Delta to Aswan. The Fourth Dynasty Egyptians traded with Byblos, on the coast of modern Lebanon, and, through the Wadi Hammamat and down the Red Sea, with the land of Punt, probably located on the African and/or Arabian coasts just outside the Bab el-Mandab (see inset).*

Ship, the skill with which it was built with a view to its eventual dismantling and reconstruction, has given strength to the argument that these ancient traders quite probably built their boats in the familiar confines of the Nile Valley, then took them apart and transported them piecemeal across the desert to Qoseir where they were reassembled for the voyage south. In any case, the Red Sea trading vessels would have been a good deal smaller, simpler and, in the event, probably more seaworthy than Cheops' Royal Ship.

But whether they were bound for the land of Punt or along the eastern Mediterranean shores or anywhere else, sea-going vessels were always known to the Egyptians as 'Byblos boats'. It seems obvious that the first ocean-going ships the Egyptians had experienced were in the trade with Byblos, the Lebanese port town that was for thousands of years the chief entrepôt of the eastern Mediterranean, where Aegean, African and Western Asiatic merchants met regularly to trade raw materials as well as finished products. Archaeological evidence from both places has established that trade existed between the Nile Valley and the Syrian coast even before the beginning of the dynastic period, but whether this trade was initiated by the Syrians or by the Egyptians is in dispute. Were the 'Byblos boats' actually Egyptian ships, or were they given that name because they had been built in Byblos by Syrian shipwrights and sailed to Egypt by 95 Syrian seamen, laden with cedar and other resinous woods that were so precious to the Egyptians?

The evidence seems to me to point more to an Egyptian origin for this extensive trade than a Syrian one. There is not much evidence for sea trade in Syrian bottoms before the Late Bronze Age, around the twelfth century BC, whereas we know that the Egyptians were expert boatmen more than a thousand years earlier. Although the early Byblites were skilled merchants, unlike their Phoenician descendants they seem never to have become sailors. Moreover, what W. A. Ward calls 'the emotional need' for the Byblos trade was entirely on the Egyptian side.[2] It was the Egyptians who wanted the precious woods and oils that were so important in their funerary cult, and while it could be argued that the Syrians' need for Egyptian gold was just as important, nonetheless the initial imperative surely came from Egypt not Syria.

The presence of cedarwood in predynastic graves confirms trade with the Lebanese coast as early as the latter part of the fourth millennium. This trade must have been sea-borne, for it is inconceivable that the Egyptians, lacking as they did both wheeled carts and heavy draft animals, could have transported large quantities of timber through territory a great part of which was hostile desert populated by often unfriendly tribes. Even if the early trade with Byblos was carried on only sporadically or in-

95 *The cedars of Lebanon near the village of Beshara in the mountains above Tripoli are all that remain of the once-majestic forests that supplied the Egyptians and other ancient peoples with resinous timbers.*

frequently, it would still have required boats that were large, stable and swift – merchantmen of a sort. We must assume that the Egyptians had such boats even as early as the last part of the fourth millennium.

If further proof were needed of the ability of Egyptian shipwrights, it is certainly provided by the Royal Ship. The size, the grace and the sophisticated technology of this craft were not produced by a people who had heretofore built nothing but rafts and dugout canoes. The Royal Ship was built by artisans who were heirs to a long, evolved tradition of ship-building and design, and although the Royal Ship itself may not have been an ocean-going vessel, nonetheless a superior technology like this must have been capable of producing seaworthy boats for long-distance journeys as well.

It has been suggested that the Royal Ship was built of cedar precisely because of the almost sacramental nature of the wood, whose use was restricted, together with that of the resins and oils extracted from it, to royalty and the gods and, by special dispensation from the king, to the nobility. But the cedars from Lebanon had a more practical attraction for the Old Kingdom ship-builders in their great size. Only in the mountains of the Lebanon could be found the enormous trees that would provide boards for a craft the size of the Royal Ship, some of whose hull timbers, we must remember, were solid pieces measuring twenty-two metres long and fourteen centimetres thick. The ships built by King Sneferu and mentioned on the Palermo Stone were each more than 100 cubits, that is more than fifty metres, long – a little longer than Cheops' ship. One of these vessels was built of cedar, the other two of a wood called 'meru', apparently another type of conifer imported to Egypt from the Syro-Lebanese coast. We must imagine that Sneferu's ships were constructed like Cheops' of huge pieces of timber scarfed and pegged and lashed together.

Because these great coniferous woods and their by-products were not available in Egypt, the Byblos trade would remain significant throughout Egyptian history. Towards the end of the Old Kingdom, late in the third millennium, when centralized authority seems to have broken down completely and somewhat anarchic conditions prevailed throughout Egypt, the wise man Ipuwer lamented the decline in trade: 'None indeed sail north to Byblos today. What can we do concerning cedarwood for our noble deceased; one used to bury the pure ones [priests? or nobles?] with its imports and one embalmed the appointees [government officials?] with its pitch in order to last....[3]

But the Byblos trade resumed,[4] and flourished. Almost a thousand years later, in the eleventh century BC, at the end of the New Kingdom when Egyptian power and influence, once dominant throughout the Middle East, had declined, a government official named Wen-Amon reported to his superiors on a trade mission to Byblos to purchase timber for the construction of 'the great and noble riverine barge of Amon-Re, King of the Gods'. Piracy, greed and hard bargaining on the part of the ruler of Byblos were only a few of the sufferings Wen-Amon detailed, but his report is interesting for our argument, indicating as it does that as long as the old beliefs and customs prevailed, that is, probably until the advent of Christianity, these coniferous woods and their resins and oils remained crucial for the Egyptians.

Navigation and the Nile

The extent of Egyptian maritime activity, so far back in ancient history, should not be surprising. 'Egypt', said Herodotus, 'is the gift of the Nile,' and if he was thinking more of agriculture than of navigation, it is nonetheless true. A traveller in Egypt today can only be struck by how valid the statement continues to be. Industry and agriculture are alike dependent on the Nile. Indeed, until very recently, the only safe, comfortable, rapid means of communication within the country was by boat along the river's seven hundred and fifty unobstructed miles from the First Cataract at Aswan to the Mediterranean Sea.

Despite many contacts with other civilizations, from earliest times the people of the Nile Valley seem to have had a linguistic and cultural unity, strung out as they were along the narrow river banks.[5] As communication developed, they attained political unity as well. The early unification of Egypt under a strong centralized authority was made possible by this slender but nearly unbreakable riverine thread of communication. The Sumerian civilization, which was developing in lower Mesopotamia at about the same time, never developed politically beyond a group of independent city states and part of the reason for this is surely geographical. Navigation and communication along the Nile were further favoured in that the prevailing wind was northerly: downriver traffic rode with the current, while the southbound traffic to Upper Egypt, going against the current, sailed before the north wind.

Some palaeobotanists have suggested that the climate of the Nile Valley, at least from around 5000 BC to the end of the Old Kingdom, was rather more humid than it has been since, with heavier, more frequent, winter rains. (Today the average annual rainfall at Cairo is two-and-a-half centimetres; in Upper Egypt it rains once every two or three years.) Extensive marshes, like the thick stands of papyrus that are often depicted in the paintings and reliefs of Old Kingdom tombs, would have spread along the Nile banks, and farther back from the river was perhaps open park-land with scattered trees – acacias, sycamores and sidders. Such trees were all useful, as we have seen from the way their wood was used for pegs and in other small details in the Royal Ship, though none of them grew to any important size. These lush marshes, rich in fish and game, were what attracted the earliest settlers to the valley, and it was presumably one of these earliest men or women who first discovered that he could venture even farther from the watery marshes out into the river

96 Boats are a characteristic motif on pottery from the Naqada II period, immediately preceding the First Dynasty. The two reed huts pictured on this example may be religious shrines, or they may have a more prosaic function. The boat represented is probably wooden rather than a papyrus raft.

itself supported by a light floating bundle of papyrus reeds. When precisely this happened we cannot even guess, for of that first primitive papyrus craft not a trace has been found. The invention of the first 'boat' may have taken place as early as the Upper Palaeolithic period, when the Nile Valley was settled by groups of hunter-gatherers moving in from the deserts to exploit the fertile river banks; and it may have been centuries after that first breakthrough that another man or woman discovered how several bundles of reeds bound together could support more than one person, could even be used to transport goods from one place to another.

The earliest abundant boat evidence that we have in Egypt is from what archaeologists call the Gerzean or Naqada II culture, immediately preceding the dynastic period. It used to be thought that the establishment of the First Dynasty represented a decisive break with the immediate predynastic past, brought on at least partly by a cultural or military invasion of the Nile Valley by outsiders who spoke a different language, worshipped other gods and travelled in distinctively different boats. That view has fewer adherents today, and students of the prehistoric period such as Elise Baumgartel[6] have shown that the Naqada II culture merges so imperceptibly into the early dynastic period that no hard and fast line can be drawn to separate them.

Characteristic of Naqada II is a skilfully made red-painted pottery covered with designs that are both naïve and at the same time often

extremely powerful. Boats appear as an important motif in this pottery, 96
so much so that they are interpreted by many archaeologists as serving
some kind of ritual or religious function: the little reed huts that are their
cabins are seen as shrines, and the figures that stand on or around the boats
are said to be participants in some fertility dance or drama, a sacred couple
or a triad, the couple with child. The theory is tempting, but we still know
very little about early religious beliefs and practices. Certainly it seems
likely that even if all the boats shown on these pots have some ritual function, they are the same kinds of boats that were used for more prosaic
purposes, fishing and transport. The evidence is of an already highly developed technology – so highly developed that a sea voyage of more than
three hundred miles from the Delta to Byblos is quite within the range
of possibility.

Landström has offered plausible reconstructions of the commonest
types of craft depicted on the pottery as well as on rock drawings in Upper
Egypt and Nubia. One type of vessel is a flat-bottomed wooden boat
made of planks stitched together with thwarts or deck beams inserted to
give the craft stability in deep water, a direct ancestor of the Royal Ship,
even if a scaled down version. The other type of boat shown on the pottery
is the papyrus raft, with its ends bound tightly together and drawn
upwards and inwards, to give the raft a stability and mobility it would
not otherwise have. Both types of boat are shown at times under sail and
at other times with a whole fringe of oars or paddles. It has been suggested
that this fringe represents the mythological 'Field of Reeds', mentioned
in the Pyramid Texts, but in the piece of painted fabric from a predynastic
grave at Gebelein that is now displayed in the Turin Museum, we can   *XI*
see unmistakably leaf-shaped oars not unlike the oars of the Royal Ship.
Some of the boats painted on pottery show similar oars.

The very earliest evidence, then, indicates that there were two parallel,
if not necessarily simultaneous, developments in Egyptian boat-building:
the raft built up of bundles of papyrus reed, and the wooden boat. The
reed raft was used with only minor variations throughout Egyptian history – as it is still used today in southern Iraq and other marshy areas
of the world. The reasons for its persistence are obvious – cheap, light,
buoyant, easy to construct, easy to replace when it falls apart, it is the
ideal work and transport vehicle in the marshes.

Reed rafts and wooden boats

In their tomb-paintings, Egyptian nobles loved to show themselves punt-
ing through the reed marshes on a light, comfortable papyrus raft, the
men hunting or fishing while the women seem to have been more content

(Opposite)

VIII A close-up view reveals how the oars are lashed to the hull.

IX Papyrus-bud finials crown the slender columns that support the cabin canopy. Cf. ill. 35.

X The cabin and central section of the ship seen from the forward port side.

simply to gaze at the lush scenery. It was a favourite form of relaxation.
Queen Meresankh III, a granddaughter of Cheops and wife of his son
97 Chephren, was painted on the walls of her Giza tomb together with her
mother, another queen, the two royal ladies standing on a graceful little
raft while they gather papyrus blossoms, a favourite decorative motif
throughout the pharaonic period. More than a thousand years later, the
98 young King Tutankhamun, in a gilt statuette from his tomb in the Valley
of the Kings, stands astride an elegant model raft, a harpoon in his raised
right arm to symbolize the ritual of the hippopotamus hunt. Despite the
ornate and rather decadent feeling of Amarna art, beneath the elaborate
gilding one detects exactly the same form and function as the raft on which
Meresankh and her mother floated a millennium earlier.

One of the loveliest of all these marsh scenes is in the Fifth Dynasty
99 mastaba of the nobleman Ti at Saqqara. The impassive official, clinging
to his staff of authority, is being punted through dense stalks of papyrus
that stand in regular vertical ranks like an impenetrable wall. But around
the static and conventionalized figure of the deceased, the artist was free
to depict the teeming luxuriance of life in the marshes, the varieties of

97 Queen Meresankh III, grand-daughter of Cheops and wife of his son Chephren, is portrayed on the wall of her tomb in the Giza necropolis, together with her mother, Hetep-heres II, in a papyrus raft, gathering flowers in the marshes – a traditional scene in tomb paintings throughout Egyptian history.

98 In this fine gilt statuette from Thebes the young King Tutankhamun stands astride a papyrus raft very like Queen Meresankh's of a thousand years earlier, except that the ends are flattened rather than upturned.

fish, crocodiles and hippopotami; high overhead the graceful papyrus-blooms nod and sway, heavy with the abundance of small birds and animals that flutter and perch amongst them. The relief has long since lost its colours, but one has nonetheless an inescapable sense of the cool greenness of these marshy depths and their appeal to the Egyptians whose actual dwelling- and work-places were more apt to be in the hot sun.

Landström says that bundles of papyrus were still being used to cross the Nile in the nineteenth century, but in Upper Egypt papyrus had died out by the Eighteenth Dynasty, though it continued to flourish in the Delta until the last century. Now it has disappeared completely as a wild plant, and with it of course have disappeared the boatwrights with the knowledge of how to build these craft. When Thor Heyerdahl, the Norwegian archaeologist-explorer, prepared a papyrus raft to carry him across the Atlantic, although the boat was built in the western desert within sight of the Giza pyramids, Heyerdahl had to import his boat-builders from Lake Chad, far away to the southeast below the Sahara Desert, and his papyrus reeds from the shores of Lake Tana in the Ethiopian highlands at the source of the Blue Nile.

The raft made of papyrus reeds continued for some time to be the only form of marine transportation available to the ancient Egyptians. One can be quite positive about this because of the later use of a two-legged mast on wooden sailboats. This kind of widespread mast, looking something like a ladder, with its very special system of rigging, was developed for use on fragile reed rafts, where the immense pressure from the mast itself, and from the big sail these boats carried, had to be distributed over as great an area as possible if the weak fibres of the boat were not to split apart. But the two-legged mast continued to be used on all types of sailing vessels right through the Old Kingdom, when it no longer served any useful function. Marine archaeologists feel that this is excellent evidence for the development of reed rafts large enough to carry heavy sails long before wooden boats came into common use.

But how and why and when did the development of wooden boats take place? Again, we can only say that it too must have been far back in antiquity, so far back in fact that its origins are lost. It must have been an entirely separate development from that of the reed raft. Boat historians such as Basil Greenhill, Director of the National Maritime Museum at Greenwich, believe that the dugout, the hollowed-out log, often with its sides extended by planking, is the origin of most types of wooden boats in the world. I do not think that this is probably true in Egypt for a number of reasons, the main one being that, from as much as we know of the Egyptian wooden boat-building tradition, it did not rely even in small craft on a keel and strakes formed of large single boards, such as would be the usual development from dugouts. Rather, because the locally available supply of hardwood was limited in length (acacia, which is a good local hardwood and was quite commonly used until very recently in Nile-side boatyards, is only available in short lengths) Egyptian boats, even those as elegant in line as the Royal Ship, were built of short lengths of wood, joined end to end and then bound along their edges. Even the central part of the boat, corresponding to the keel, was built up of segments. In the Royal Ship this 'keel plank', as Lionel Casson calls it, was made of eight shorter pieces of timber.

Herodotus described Egyptian boat-building in the fifth century BC, and it had probably not changed much over the previous two thousand years: 'From the acacia tree they cut planks three feet long, which they put together like courses of brick, building up the hull as follows: they join these three-foot lengths together with long, close-set dowels; when they have built up a hull in this fashion [out of the planks] they stretch cross-beams over them. They use no ribs, and they caulk seams from the inside using papyrus fibres. They fashion a single steering oar and this they pass through the keel. They use masts of acacia and sails of papyrus.'[7]

(Opposite)

99 As we have seen (ill. 19) the raft-in-the-marshes motif was by no means restricted to royalty; nobles too enjoyed hunting and fishing from reed boats. Here the Fifth Dynasty nobleman Ti commands his followers in a relief from his Saqqara tomb.

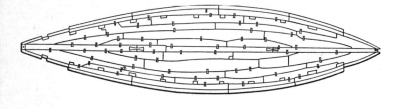

100, 101 *The boats discovered at Dahshur in 1893 were thought by their excavator to have been part of the burial equipment of the Twelfth Dynasty king, Sesostris III, but doubt has since been cast on this attribution. The strakes drawing of one of the two boats now in the Cairo Museum (above) shows its similarities with – and its differences from – the Royal Ship of Cheops. Note the narrow central plank in three sections joined by dovetail clamps. The Dahshur boats had no frames and relied on deck beams or thwarts to maintain their rigidity. The third surviving boat (below) is today in the Field Museum of Natural History, Chicago. The metal bands to support the hull are a modern addition.*

100, 101

  This technique of boat-building is best exemplified in the Dahshur boats, which had been buried near the pyramid of Sesostris III, although it has never been entirely clear whether they were actually part of the king's burial equipment or that of some lesser dignitary from one of the many other burials in the neighbourhood. A sledge found near the boats was assumed to have been used to transport them, together with their contents, from the edge of the river or floodplain to the pyramid site south of Saqqara, where they were placed apparently within a large mud-brick vault outside the south temenos wall of the pyramid area. Two of these boats are in the Cairo Museum, and one is at the Field Museum of Natural History in Chicago. There were three (or perhaps more) other boats, but in such poor condition that they could not be preserved. Landström, who has studied the Cairo boats, says that they are made of wood that had been used earlier for other purposes. Is it really possible, he asks, that 'the most powerful King of the Middle Kingdom should have been borne to his grave in such a wretched craft?'

  But the question of the ownership of the Dahshur boats need not concern us here. What is of greater importance is the way in which they were constructed, which is precisely as Herodotus had described. Short lengths of wood (Ahmed Fakhry says it is cedar, but even that is uncertain) are joined along their edges with little butterfly or hourglass wooden clamps that are set into the wood from the inside. Apparently, unlike the Royal Ship, no lashing or sewing was used. It seems incredible that the planking could have held together in water by means of these rather simple clamps. As in the Royal Ship, the hull was built up around a central plank instead of a proper keel; this plank was made of three or four sections of wood joined at the ends with dovetail clamps that were somewhat larger than those used in the rest of the ship. Unlike the Royal Ship, there were no frames inserted into the hull, but thwarts or deck beams running across the ship at the level of the gunwales gave it rigidity. These beams were pegged to the hull planking with dowels. The deck itself was probably laid in removable hatches over the deck beams, like the deck on the Royal Ship. The timbers used were all of uneven lengths, and one does indeed get the impression that the builders grabbed whatever lay to hand and fitted it in wherever it would go. In his report, the excavator, Jacques de Morgan, said that one of these boats was painted white, another red, and that both had multi-coloured ornaments, but not a trace of this painting can be seen today. The Cairo boats are in a fairly neglected condition in any case, which may account for Landström's description of them as 'wretched'.

Landström has also pointed out, in the Middle Kingdom tomb of the official Khnum-hotep at Beni Hasan, an example of such a boat under construction. Five men are working on the boat while a sixth, perhaps a foreman by the cut of his garment, is looking on. Landström believes that the boat's planking is being sewn together by the second workman from the left who appears to be drawing bindings tight. In any case, it is definitely a question of short pieces of wood that are being joined together like bricks, as Herodotus said, and at least in this case they are a good deal more regular than the pieces used in the Dahshur boats. Above this scene, two carpenters are working, one pulling his saw through an upright plank, and the other using an adze of a sort similar to the one in the boat-building scene below. This tool seems to have been an all-purpose implement in ancient Egypt, for it is shown over and over again in drawings and reliefs, and is often part of burial equipment, even for so exalted a being as the king.

The ship-building scene was a favourite motif, like sowing the grain or the birth of calves, that occurred repeatedly in the reliefs and wall-paintings of later Old Kingdom tombs, where officials and nobles set out with pride not just their own public achievements but the rich ordinariness of their everyday lives. In the same Fifth Dynasty mastaba of Ti as the marsh scene described above, another relief shows different types of boats *102* being constructed, each type obviously to serve a different purpose. The boat on the right side of the middle register has rounded ends, that on the left has one end (the stern?) sharply pointed and the other abruptly chopped off. The boat in the lowest register is the most interesting for us, for, as we have seen, this is the same shape as the hull of the Royal Ship with the papyriform stem and stern posts removed. We know of a number of these ships from reliefs of the Fifth Dynasty, most of them

102 The Fifth Dynasty mastaba tomb of Ti (see ill. 99) has also provided us with this scene – until the discovery and reconstruction of the Royal Ship one of our few clues to ancient methods of ship-building.

shown under sail though there are a few with the mast lowered and the oarsmen at work. As was noted above in the chapter on the reconstruction of the boat, it has been proposed that papyriform boats were more often than not ordinary river travelling boats on to which the papyriform pieces were socketed, as they were on the Royal Ship, to transform it into a boat for a special occasion.

In the Ti reliefs, the adze in several sizes is, again, the all-purpose tool, used ubiquitously for shaping and smoothing. Another almost equally useful is a long hammering tool, shaped like a bat. The saw on the right in the lowest register, one writer has pointed out, is a pull-saw, deriving its thrust from being pulled towards the sawyer rather than, as with modern saws, being pushed away. In the bottom register workmen are attaching the bulwark to a nearly completed hull and we can see the tenons of the mortise-and-tenon joints that will secure the bulwark to the sheer-strake. In the scene above, a workman, perhaps a foreman, between the two boats is holding a ferrule and lead with which to check the accuracy of the hull curves.

Unfortunately there is not much evidence, in either pictures or text, of the initial stages of boat-building. But the making of boats is a conservative occupation, particularly in rural parts of the world where boats are more often than not made by the men who sail them and who hand the tradition on to each succeeding generation, from father to son. Boats and boat-making are very slow to change. It seems safe to assume, then, that ancient Egyptian boats were made much as the edge-joined, shell-built, sewn boats are constructed today in the few places, such as southern Arabia and Bangladesh, where they are still being built. These modern boats all seem to be built around a keel while the Egyptian boats, as we have seen, had no keel until probably some time in the New Kingdom.

Both the Royal Ship and the Dahshur boats were built up around the central keel plank that was formed of several smaller pieces of wood. A *100* glance at the strakes drawings will show that, in the Dahshur boats this *81* keel plank was a long narrow dividing piece, whereas in the Royal Ship it was a good deal wider and virtually formed the entire flat bottom of the craft. In the Royal Ship, the eight timbers of the keel plank were probably laid first, joined at their ends and along the edges. Then the forward and after sections were raised and shored up to give the proper curvature to the hull. As the sides were built up, they were supported from the outside by moulds or buttresses of some sort. Greenhill describes the building of a similar craft in Bangladesh, 'surrounded by a forest of struts and guylines holding the planks in tension'. Once the side planks had been raised, frames were sometimes, though not always, inserted to strengthen the hull, and then the deck beams were laid across the central 'spine', the narrow shelf or stringer that ran from bow to stern down the length of the ship.

In a series of wall-paintings from a tomb at Zawiyet el-Meitin, according to André Servin, the French historian who studied ancient Egyptian ships and their construction, we can see workmen with hatchet-like axes carving out what appears to be the central stringer ('le longeron central du pont'). Servin was mistaken about a number of features, but although he was writing some years before the discovery of the Royal Ship, his description of the interior structure of the boats in the Zawiyet el-Meitin painting as well as others from the Old Kingdom, is remarkably close to the actual structure that was revealed by Cheops' craft. In Servin's drawing, the central stringer rests on stanchions spaced at intervals, and supports the deck beams, exactly as it does in the Royal Ship.

One of the paintings at Zawiyet el-Meitin showed six workers twisting levers in order to tighten a rope truss that arches over the boat from bow to stern. Servin thought they were drawing up bow and stern to achieve the proper sheer for the craft, but it has been pointed out that no hull could withstand this kind of strain without bursting the seams. Landström says such trusses represent a stage in construction, a support for the unfinished hull, like Greenhill's 'forest of struts and guylines', that will be removed when the boat is finished.

We know these hogging trusses from finished boats as well, where they are used to give greater flexibility to ships that must travel in heavy seas, often laden with cargo. The double rope runs from bow to stern, in fact loops over both bow and stern. A stick, inserted between the two strands of the double rope and twisted, would tighten the cable and thus help to maintain the sheer of the boat and keep her from breaking up in heavy weather. Another type, the girdle truss, was sometimes used instead of, or in conjunction with, the hogging truss. This consisted of two ropes that encircled the hull above the waterline. A third rope was woven or laced between them in such a manner that strain on the hull timbers could be counteracted by tightening the girdle to hold them together.

At Abusir, just north of Saqqara, in the mortuary temple of King Sahure, one of the early rulers of the Fifth Dynasty, were once the remains of a wonderful series of reliefs showing the departure and subsequent arrival home again of a merchant fleet of twelve big ships, doubtless in the Syrian trade to judge by the number of Asiatics, recognizable by their long hair and beards, on board the returning vessels. These ships all have hogging trusses and many have girdle trusses as well, so they have obviously been used to transport heavy cargoes over long distances. The same hogging trusses can be seen in the painted reliefs of Queen Hatshepsut's temple at Deir el-Bahri, where the Eighteenth Dynasty queen's merchant

103

fleet is shown upon its return from a successful voyage to Punt; on another wall are the huge hog-trussed barges that transported a pair of giant obelisks, each weighing about 2,400 tons, for the queen from Aswan to Thebes.

104

The papyriform boat

As we have seen, the Royal Ship is neither a papyrus raft nor an ordinary wooden boat, but a papyriform boat, a wooden boat that was deliberately built in the shape of a huge raft made of papyrus bundles. Landström distinguishes this type as early as the Badarian period, that is, about six thousand years ago, in a ceramic model boat. Already, then, if we accept his evidence, in the fourth millennium there were at least three distinctive kinds of boats: simple reed rafts, probably used primarily for hunting or sport within the marshes but rarely on the broad reaches of the river itself; wooden boats, faster and more stable than the lightweight rafts, most likely used for riverine travel and transport but that would later on in their sturdier versions be commandeered for long-distance ocean voyages; and papyriform boats that were built with the same technology as the wooden river-boats but for some reason in a deliberate, if more elaborate, imitation of the shape of papyrus rafts. The papyriform boats seem always to have been used in connection with some cult or religious purpose, as pilgrimage or funeral or burial boats or perhaps to transport the king or the image of a god or goddess. The point about all this is that the Royal Ship of King Cheops is not a development or evolution from papyrus rafts. Rafts, as both Landström and Greenhill have pointed

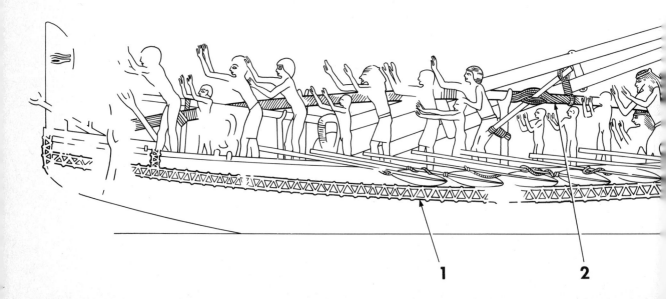

1   2

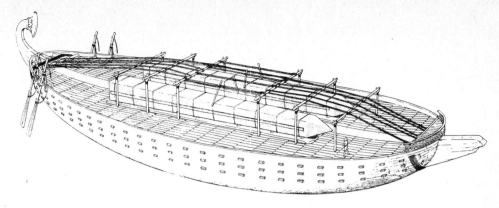

104 The Eighteenth Dynasty queen Hatshepsut shipped two enormous obelisks – each about 2,400 tons – from the quarry site at Aswan downriver to Thebes. A modern reconstruction of the barge, based on reliefs in Hatshepsut's temple at Deir el-Bahri, clearly shows how a hogging truss was passed beneath bow and stern to prevent them from collapsing under the tremendous weight.

out, are a dead-end development in maritime history; that is, they did not evolve into anything else. No matter how big you make it, or to what extent you build up its sides, a raft is still a raft, deriving its buoyancy from the lightness of the material used, whether lightweight wood or reed, while a boat is buoyant because it encloses a volume that is as light as, or lighter than, the volume of water it displaces. Boats change and develop according to the uses to which they are put, the climate and waterways they must deal with. Despite its papyriform shape, then, the developments that led to the Cheops ship came from wooden boats rather than from papyrus rafts.

103 One of the ships depicted on the walls of King Sahure's mortuary temple at Abusir, the Fifth Dynasty complex just north of Saqqara. Note the girdle truss (1) around the hull, and the hogging truss (2) with a stick for tightening the ropes so that the boat could be made more rigid in heavy seas and less likely to ship water.

105 *An early model of a papyriform boat, no longer a royal ship, but already, by the Sixth Dynasty, an example of how nobles were beginning to assume burial privileges formerly connected only with royalty. The four little seated figures facing aft are oarsmen and the figure facing them may be the helmsman or captain of the ship.*

THE PAPYRIFORM BOAT

106, 107 (Below and opposite above) *The funeral and/or pilgrimage boat of Chancellor Meketre (Eleventh Dynasty), from his tomb at Thebes, is one of a pair (cf. colour ill. XII). The mast and rigging of this vessel indicate that it was intended to be propelled by sail on an upriver journey. The shape of bow and stern, and the papyrus-bud finials on the columns, are very reminiscent of Cheops' Royal Ship.*

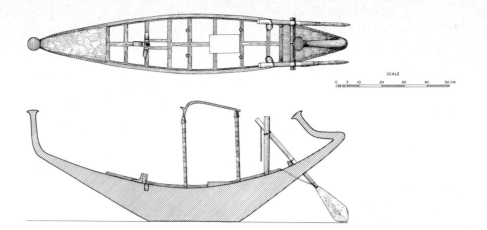

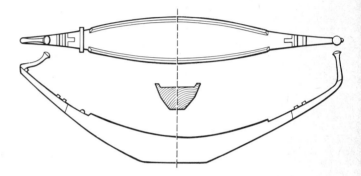

108 Queen Neith in the late Sixth Dynasty was buried with a number of fine large boat models, including the papyriform model shown here in plan and section. Despite the exaggerated sheer, the profile is very like that of Cheops' Royal Ship.

109 (Below) In a late relief, temple priests are shown bearing aloft a sacred papyriform funerary barque.

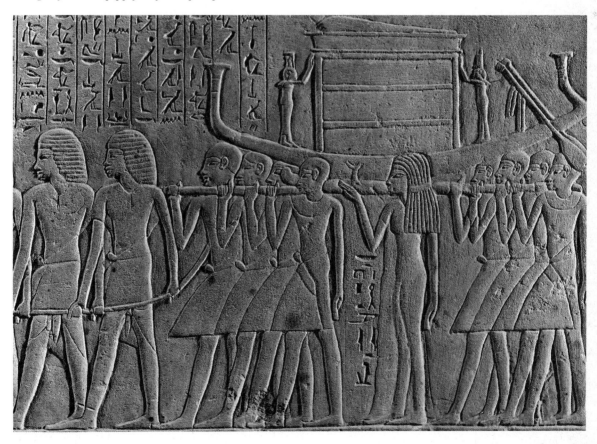

The particular form of the Royal Ship, with its straight vertical prow and the stern post drawn back in a graceful curve over the after quarters of the ship, can be traced back to the rock drawings of boats that have been found in Upper Egypt and Nubia, though it is not clear whether these outline drawings represent papyrus rafts or papyriform boats. Landström believes that the papyriform shape was restricted to royalty, at least during the Old Kingdom. Certainly during that period, and even later, the models and relief carvings that are associated with royal burials show the same elegant and graceful profile as King Cheops' ship. Other depictions show what are also clearly papyriform boats, but the fore and aft overhangs are treated differently, especially during the Old Kingdom, as *105* we can see in the Sixth Dynasty model from a tomb at Aswan. But even if one concludes that the shape was restricted to royalty during the Old Kingdom, by the Middle Kingdom, like so much else of the royal burial ritual and funerary paraphernalia, the papyriform shape seems to have been taken over for use by the nobility, as we can see from the fine *106, 107* Eleventh Dynasty models of papyriform boats that were found in the *XII* tomb of Meketre at Deir el-Bahri.

In the mortuary temple of King Sahure's pyramid complex at Abusir *58* were found the ruins of a delicately carved relief of a papyriform ship that, except for the fact that it is under sail, could be a drawing in stone of the Royal Ship of King Cheops. All we can see unfortunately is the prow of the ship and the figures of a few sailors, with the great billow of the huge sail, decorated like damascene with a pattern of framed rosettes in the fine relief work that was typical of the Fifth Dynasty. The prow has a more finished appearance than the one on Cheops' ship, topped as it is by a half-open papyrus bud and the disc of the Sun-god. (By the Fifth Dynasty, under the increasing influence of the priests of Heliopolis, the Sun-god seems to have become much more important than during the Fourth Dynasty.) The prow of Sahure's Ship of State, as it is called, has the same elegant lift as Cheops', and the little baldachin on the foredeck

is matched by the one on the Royal Ship. The *wedjat*-eye, the all-seeing eye of the hawk-headed god Horus, was painted on the prow as a talisman against evil.

Large papyriform models were buried together with other model boats near the Saqqara pyramid of the Sixth Dynasty queen Neith. Neith was the daughter of Pepi I and wife of the long-lived Pepi II, who reigned for about ninety years. Queen Neith's papyriform boats also had the same profile as the Royal Ship, although they had such an exaggerated sheer that the midships section of the craft would have been awash had they ever been floated.

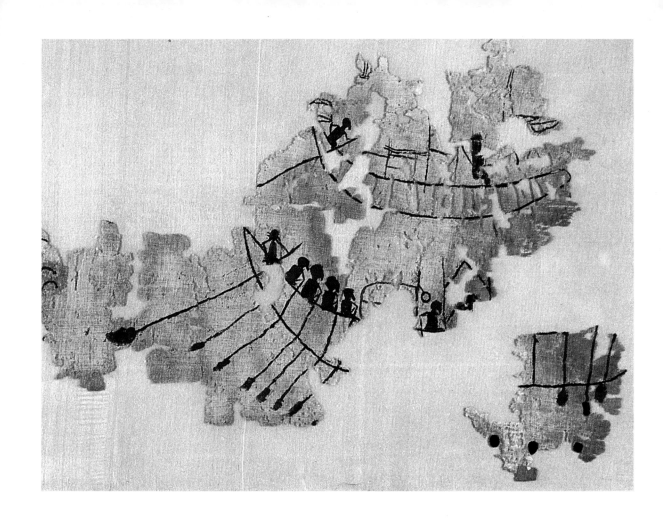

The shape of the papyriform craft survived virtually unchanged throughout Egyptian history. Tutankhamun's model boats are similar to the Royal Ship of Cheops, and Queen Hatshepsut's stately ship, carved on the walls of her temple at Deir el-Bahri, is like it too, except for the fact that both bow and stern posts are curved back over the hull and an elegant baldachin arches over the high throne amidships. A similar type of ship was used in late New Kingdom times as the barque of the god, not just of the Sun-god alone but of various other gods as well. These barques rested on carrying platforms, so that they could be borne aloft by the priesthood during religious ceremonies such as the Feast of the Valley, when the Barque of Amon was taken from the temple at Karnak and displayed in processions at the other temples of Thebes.

XIII

109

Contemporary with the royal and religious ships, we know of dozens, perhaps hundreds, of models from private tombs of papyriform funerary or pilgrimage ships, and it is in these that we see the greatest variety of shapes. Private artists, lacking the skill of court artisans and at the same time not so strictly bound by conventions and traditions, were free within certain limits to produce whatever they wished, and the fancies of private patrons must often have influenced their ideas as well. Thus in the British Museum, for example, we find the eloquent simplicity of a Twelfth Dynasty model together with the crudeness of a papyriform sailboat, where the woodworker has mistakenly reversed the stem and stern posts! Most of the oldest examples are shown with one or more rudders or steering-oars and by the Middle Kingdom these are slung through rudder posts that are often decorated with the hawk-heads of the god Horus. With the exception of Sahure's Ship of State, few of the boats are sailboats; more often they are shown with oars or, if oarless, they are perhaps intended to be towed, either by other boats or from the shore. Many of the little model boats show the mummy of the deceased seated in a chair or lying on a bier beneath the central baldachin, often accompanied by priests and mourners. These boats might represent the journey of the mummified body to its final resting-place; or the soul's voyage into the afterlife; or a pilgrimage to the holy places of Egypt that would be part of the funeral rite. Or, in a synthesis that would not be uncharacteristic of ancient Egyptian belief, with its remarkable interpenetration of reality and myth, the literal and the symbolic, the boats could symbolize all of these things simultaneously.

110

111

Why these boats took a papyriform shape, and why they should be part of a king's burial equipment, are questions that we have barely touched on. But before we can consider the answers, we must take a brief look at Old Kingdom religious beliefs, if only to make more comprehensible the terms of reference within which the papyriform boats must fit.

(Opposite)

XIII The magnificent late New Kingdom 'Papyrus of Anhai' depicts Nun, the god of the primeval waters, lifting up the boat of the rising sun.

110 A model funerary barque from the Middle Kingdom shows the owner's mummy lying in state beneath a canopy supported by lotus-blossom columns. The Horus hawk-heads on the rudder columns are a rather crude approximation of what may have been intended for the Royal Ship.

111 In another example of a model from a private tomb the woodworker has mistakenly switched the papyriform bow and stern posts.

CHAPTER SEVEN

Death, religion and survival

The Nile: flood and fertility

The great drama of the annual Nile flood has been missing from Egyptian life since the construction near the First Cataract at Aswan of a series of water controls culminating in the High Dam which was inaugurated by President Nasser in 1970. Even today, however, with the dam and Lake Nasser behind it to steady the river's impressive surge, the normally rapid flow has slowed noticeably by the middle of May, and the water in the irrigation canals, whose interlacing network lends a tropical lushness to what would otherwise be desert, is a murky, stagnant and unhealthy brew. It is easy to imagine, then, what it must have been like each year when the great river was reduced to a sluggish creek, and all Egypt waited anxiously for a sign that the water would soon begin to rise again.

94

By mid-June the river begins to change. Far off in Africa, 1,500 miles away in the highlands of Ethiopia and in the formidable, fetid marshes of the Sudd below the Mountains of the Moon, the two sources of the Nile, the Blue and the White, quicken with the rich, silt-laden run-off from spring rains in the mountains. In other times the rise was sudden and dramatic, from one day to the next. Lucie Duff Gordon observed it in Luxor in 1864. 'The Nile is rising fast,' she wrote in a letter home dated 12 June, 'and a star of most fortunate character has made its appearance – so Youssef tells me – and portends a good year and an end to our afflictions.' That star, observed by Lady Duff Gordon's Upper Egyptian peasant friend in the 1860s, was the same Sothis or Sirius, the Dog Star, whose annual re-appearance in the dawn sky just before sunrise heralded for the ancient Egyptians the beginning of the Nile flood and the start of the solar New Year. This heliacal rising, as it is called, of Sirius was awaited with anxiety, for on the success or failure of the Nile flood depended Egypt's very existence. Too much was as threatening as too little (the afflictions referred to by Lady Duff Gordon had been caused by an exceptionally high flood the previous year that had drowned crops and animals, as well as humans). Those years, extremely rare though they were, when the flood failed altogether, were greeted rightly enough as national, indeed cosmic, calamities.

It is curious then that the ancient Egyptians seem never to have worshipped the Nile directly as a god or power or spirit. The Nile was often personified as Hapi, the strange old man with pendulous breasts, but this rather weird figure seems to have been a symbol only, perhaps a demiurge, without religious significance. It is true, as the American Egyptologist James Breasted pointed out, that the god Osiris in his fertility aspect was identified with the life-giving waters of the Nile. But the Nile, as we shall *112* see, was only one among many sources of the fertility of Osiris. Vital as the Nile's flood was to Egypt's survival, its role in religion seems to have been restricted to an area of sympathetic magic very close to the charms still practised by the fellahin, whose lives depend on the great river even today.

Religion and the rhythm of life

If it is difficult for us to appreciate what life was really like in ancient Egypt, it is almost impossible for us to comprehend the religion of these people who lived in such intimate symbiosis with the world around them. Nonetheless, before we can understand why King Cheops, like other Egyptians earlier and later, buried his great ship (and probably others like it) next to his tomb, we must look at what we can discern of Egyptian beliefs about life and death and survival in the hereafter.

'Religion' at first appears too dignified a word for such a primitive mishmash of competing totems, animal-headed gods, and inconsistent, confusing, in fact conflicting mythologies. The modern mind draws back in dismay, embarrassed by the superficial aspects of Egyptian belief. Yet we are compelled to admit that these same beliefs persisted for at least four thousand years of human culture, that they were a source of comfort in the face of death and of moral assurance when confronted with life's problems. It was a system that endured and continued to sustain its adherents until the coming of Christianity which, in its redeeming aspects, had a legitimate Egyptian precursor in the Osirian faith.

As we have seen in previous chapters, the earliest Egyptians were an intelligent and energetic people, capable, within their limited means, of sophisticated feats of technology, and gifted with an artistic sensibility that is borne out in poetry as much as it is in stone. That they had a profound understanding of the relationship between earth and the heavens is obvious from the alignment of their monuments to the cardinal points, to the pole star, to the seasonal solstices. We also have incontrovertible evidence, from as early as the beginning of the dynastic period, of their

112 Osiris, god of the underworld, was one of the few Egyptian gods invariably portrayed as anthropomorphic and as a mummy – here shown in traditional pose wearing the Atef-crown and carrying the crook and flail in a late New Kingdom wall-painting from Thebes.

concern to find an underlying principle, a rightness and order at the heart of things that would guarantee justice not as a moral principle, but as an expression of divine will. If the philosophy is one that has so far eluded modern minds, the fault lies not with the ancients but rather with ourselves.

Of course, along with the sophisticated theology went a good deal of primitive magic. One of the most appealing aspects of ancient Egyptian religion is the way these two co-exist side by side, a charm to ward off snakes or scorpions next to a deeply moving hymn to the regenerative powers of the sun. Perhaps part of the failure of modern religion, its inability to answer to the needs of modern life, lies in the way we have separated theology from folk belief. For the Egyptians, there was no such separation: magic and superstition went hand in hand with the most sophisticated speculation.

To understand the background of Egyptian religion we must look at Egypt's peculiar geography and climate. The geographical isolation imposed by the vast and hostile deserts that enclose the narrow river valley meant not only a cultural isolation, the opportunity to develop what was an almost totally indigenous culture with rare incursions from outside, but also a freedom from invasion that was most unusual in the ancient world. A brief glance at the destruction levels of any other Early Bronze Age culture in the Middle East will confirm the woeful tale. In Mesopotamia, in Syria-Palestine, in Anatolia, towns and city states erected massive walls to protect themselves, only to have them smashed and burned by invaders over and over again. Life was precarious and often terrifying. The Egyptians avoided all this. Only in the upper reaches of the Nile, on the borders with Nubia, did they build fortified towns, and these were not so much towns as garrisoned trading posts to protect traffic along the Nile. The Egyptians were free from the overriding fear that dominated other cultures. Their geography, moreover, made possible from very early on a strongly centralized authority that contributed to their sense of security, as we have seen. Communication with the outside world was difficult; communication within Egypt, along the Nile, was swift and easy, as easy as raising sail or setting to the oars. With a good following wind, a message despatched from the court at Memphis could reach important posts in Upper Egypt within a week.

The rainless desert climate, moreover, added to the Egyptian's sense of ease with his environment. Day after day, without fail, the sun rose, crossed the cloudless heavens, and set, to rise once again the following day. Rainfall was negligible, storms almost non-existent; yet the terrible life of the true desert was unknown here in the river valley where, during the spring and summer seasons, abundant water combined with heat and sunlight and the annual deposit of silt, to create a rich, fertile land. In the cultures to the north and east of Egypt, nature was a terrible, unpredictable force to be reckoned with, a jealous god of the desert or steppe, to be placated with prayer and sacrifice, before whom humankind was weak and powerless. In the valley of the Nile, despite the occasional failure of the flood, nature was seen as the Egyptian's partner in an ordered and beneficent universe.

113 Seen here supported by the king, the little seated figure of the goddess Ma'et, crowned with ostrich plumes, represented the essential and unchanging rightness and order of the universe.

It has often been said that the ancient Egyptians lacked a sense of history, and to a certain extent this is true, especially during the Old Kingdom. The daily rhythm of the sun, the regularity of the river's flood or the seasons, imposed this feeling: things had always been so, would always be so. History implies change, but life for the ancient Egyptian was unchanging and orderly. The role of the king as god, or as god's representative, was to maintain that order. There is a curious little figure in the Egyptian pantheon, a kneeling female with a characteristic feather on her head, whom we call the goddess Ma'et, though she seems less a goddess in fact *113* than a symbol for an important concept. Our translation of the concept of *ma'et* is tentative at best, for there is no one word in European languages to convey it: truth, justice, order, righteousness (but righteousness implies a strictly moral judgment that is missing from this idea). Rundle Clark, in *Myth and Symbol in Ancient Egypt*, describes how, at the end of the daily temple service, the officiating priest would raise the little figure of Ma'et before the god's image, as a re-assertion of the unchanging rightness and order of the universe and of the god's responsibility for maintaining it. Perhaps the best interpretation of the concept is in this sense of the unchanging persistence of things-as-they-are. It is difficult for us to appreciate a value judgment that has nothing to do with good or evil, but solely with a sense of universal order, not as something towards which we strive, but as something that *is*, and that *is* yesterday as it *is* tomorrow, unhistorical, unchanging, without past or future.

This changeless world was an ideal that was not always achieved. Even in the early dynasties we can detect evidence of internal conflicts, and later, after the collapse of the Sixth Dynasty, there was a period between the Old and Middle Kingdoms, called by historians the First Intermediate Period, that, though brief in time, was characterized by a feudalistic reversion to local control. The lack of centralized order was perceived by later

Egyptians as an intolerable state of affairs and remembered with fear and loathing.

Death and discontinuity

The sphere in which the Egyptian did most clearly experience change was the one common to all humanity: death. Concerned as he was with order and continuity, death came as the great interruption, and the comprehension of death, the need somehow to incorporate the fact of death in the unchanging order of the universe, was central to his religious belief. To us, the ancient Egyptian appears obsessed with death; yet, we should rather think of him as obsessed with life's continuity. His deepest concern was survival, not just of the individual (and least of all during the period with which we are dealing), but of the whole order and structure of the perceived world – sun, moon and stars, the ebb and flow of the Nile, the passage of the seasons, the fertility of crops, animals and humans.

Intimately related to the preservation of the world's order was the institution of kingship, not just the political institution, in itself an unchanging and eternal phenomenon, but the king as an individual personality as well. A vigorous debate has long been waged among Egyptologists as to whether the king was actually thought of as a god, or as a representative of the gods, or as an intercessor between humanity and the divine, a sort of glorified chief priest. Most Egyptologists feel that the king certainly became a god after his death (though there are some strong arguments against this view) and it seems that, during the Old Kingdom, he was seen as something very like a god during his lifetime, at least at certain crucial ceremonial moments such as the *hebsed* jubilee, a magic ritual to restore the king's flagging powers and vitality. But whether he was actually worshipped as a god or not, the king was certainly the guarantor of *ma'et*, of that order and stability and rightness of things-as-they-are. The two concepts, *ma'et* and the kingship, were thus intimately connected.

The crisis in this relationship came with the death of the king. Despite its inevitability, the king's death was viewed with alarm as a threat to the established order – not just to the political order of government, but to the whole cosmic order of the universe. It was a moment of almost unbearable psychological tension. The earliest documents attest to the profound distress that was evoked by an event of such cataclysmic import. 'Sky rains, stars darken, The vaults quiver, earth's bones tremble, The planets stand still,' Utterance 273 of the Pyramid Texts tells us.[1]

By the time King Zoser had built his Step Pyramid at Saqqara in the Third Dynasty, and probably much earlier, an elaborate funerary ritual had already been developed to protect against this threatened incoherence of the universe. Part of that ritual, as it was performed for the actual burial rites of the kings of the Pyramid Age, was described in chapter two. We can imagine that the burial service itself was preceded by days, if not weeks or months, of ceremony and ritual. (In the tomb of Queen Mere-sankh III at Giza, 272 days is mentioned as the period of time between death and interment, but this may be exceptionally long.) The ritual would have been carried out in the greatest secrecy in order to protect the ruler in his weak and powerless condition. A faultless performance of the ceremonies was necessary to ensure the continuation of the king-ship, both in the hereafter to which the dead king proceeded, and in the here-and-now where the kingship continued in the person of the heir to the throne, maintaining and guaranteeing the order and stability of *ma'et*. Interestingly, the heir seems not to have assumed the throne directly on his predecessor's death but only after the conclusion of the long burial ceremonies. There could not be two kings, and the first was not well and truly gone until he had been ceremonially despatched.

At this early stage in Egyptian history, as far as we can tell, mummifica-tion was used only on the bodies of members of the royal family. The oldest mummified body known is said to have been found in a Fifth Dynasty grave at Meidum by the British archaeologist Flinders Petrie. (The mummy, which was sent to England, was destroyed in the bombing of London in 1944.) But even during earlier dynasties, efforts had been made to preserve bodies by wrapping them in linen soaked in resins from the fragrant woods of Syria and perhaps from the land of Punt as well. No king's mummy has yet been found from the Old Kingdom, but the mummified viscera of Queen Hetep-heres were found by Reisner buried in an alabaster container in a niche close by the queen's empty alabaster sarcophagus. Some of the embalming fluid can still be seen in the bottom of the container.

Reisner's speculations about the reasons for Queen Hetep-heres' secret secondary burial near her son's pyramid at Giza (see chapter two) were based on his knowledge of the tremendous importance Egyptians attached to the preservation of the body after death and the fear and loathing that were evoked by its desecration. The body was the repository of the ani-mating spirit of the personality, which had two separate and quite dif-ferent aspects. The *ba*, represented by a little bird with a bearded human *114* head, is usually translated as 'soul'. Released from the body at death, the bird-soul could move back and forth between the body in its tomb and the world outside (it is often depicted fluttering in the shaft of the tomb) as well as in the transcendent world of the stars above. The stars were sometimes thought of as the souls of the deceased, so many little *ba*-birds clutching lamps in their beaks.

A more complicated concept is that of the *ka*, also confusingly often translated as 'soul', but in a more general sense as a vital animating spirit. The *ka*, which was created at birth, was shown hieroglyphically as two
115 arms extending upward, symbolizing a protective embrace. In that sense it represents a beneficent power that can be transmitted from one being to another, from a god to a mortal (usually the king), from the king to his subjects, or, interestingly, from father to son. As Horus inherits the *ka* of his father Osiris, so the king inherits his father's *ka*, the power of the kingship.

114 (Above) The 'ba' or soul of the deceased was depicted as a bird with a human face, often carrying a lantern. Here the 'ba' hovers over a mummified body, recalling how Isis fluttered her wings over Osiris to re-animate him.

115 The 'ka', symbolized by a pair of arms held out in protective embrace, is like 'ba' often translated as soul – but more in the sense of the vital, animating spirit of a personality.

The period between an individual's death and interment was referred to as the time when his or her *ka* was 'at rest'. The Egyptians then had good reason for the anxiety they felt at the death of the king, for the king's *ka*, the power that maintained order or *ma'et*, was temporarily absent from the universe. Once the ceremony of interment had been completed, the *ka* could return to the body. Without the body, the *ka* had no way to receive the offerings, prayers and rituals that were to benefit the deceased in his tomb chapel. This was the real reason for the importance of the body's preservation: without it, there was no home for the *ka*.

The cults of Osiris and Re-Atum

From the very beginning of Egyptian history, that is, at least from the First Dynasty, we can find traces of the two cults, the one of Osiris and the other of the Sun-god Re-Atum in his many aspects, that had impressed themselves on the Egyptian psychology, obviously answering to the deep anxieties Egyptians felt about the great question of death, especially the king's death. Of the two cults, that of Osiris is more accessible to our *112* minds, both because it is more logically coherent as a group of legends, and because it relates closely to the whole eastern Mediterranean phenomenon of the fertility or corn god, whose death and rebirth in some sense redeems humankind from the terrible finality of our own deaths. It was once fashionable among Egyptologists to see the two cults in opposition, if not in outright conflict – a conflict that could be related in historical terms to the political ascendancy of various priesthoods. The sun-cult was said to be exclusive and royal, a religion of the educated intellectual classes, while the Osirian was a people's religion, emotional, appealing to the heart rather than to the intellect, and democratic, in the sense that it was said to have guaranteed access to the afterlife to whoever followed the prescribed rules of behaviour and ritual, rather than solely to royalty.

This theory of a conflict is a little too neat to fit the facts such as we now know them. It seems more likely that although there was a certain amount of tension between the two cults, they were conceived of as complementary ways of expressing the same reality rather than antagonistic and opposing versions of the truth.

The king when he died became the Sun-god or part of the god's entourage that crossed the sky with him in his boat; he also became Osiris. It is a mistake to see two separate views or even two separate sets of symbols. For the ancient Egyptians, both were valid simultaneously, in a particular and actual way. Moreover, the dead king was also present in his tomb, where he received the daily offerings and prayers and the seasonal

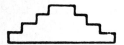

116 *The hieroglyph representing the Primeval Mound, the first piece of earth to emerge from the watery chaos at the creation – strikingly like King Zoser's Third Dynasty Step Pyramid at Saqqara (ill. 12).*

rituals that were presented to him. Again we come up against the Egyptian habit of perceiving what appear to be separate realities, or conflicting aspects of reality, with no sense of disharmony, and again we must be wary of approaching this ancient, non-logical perception with our insatiable need to categorize and systematize.

The collection of some seven hundred magic spells, hymns, prayers, incantations and fragments of mythology that Egyptologists call the Pyramid Texts were intended to assist the dead ruler on his dangerous journey to the hereafter, and to secure his happiness and well-being once arrived there. The Texts were found inscribed in long lines of hieroglyphs, filled with once brightly coloured pigments and carved on the internal walls of the pyramids of the kings and queens of the Fifth and Sixth Dynasties. The texts are vivid and dramatic in their imagery, and often fraught with emotion. There are three main stages on the voyage to resurrection: awakening in the dark tomb where, in a conjunction of mythology and actuality, the king's body must be protected by spells against the snakes and scorpions that inhabit such places; the ascent or crossing to heaven, over the water that separates earth from sky, by bribing or threatening or pleading with the ferryman; and, finally, the joyous admission to the company of the gods and the great god, the Sun-god himself. At times the dead king is identified as the son of Re-Atum, sharing in the Sun-god's power; at other times he is said to ride as a passenger in the sun's boat, or he is a member of the god's entourage, his amanuensis or secre-

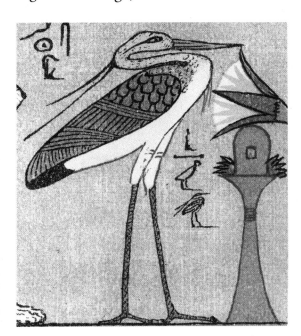

117 *As one of the representations of the Sun-god, the phoenix bird, here depicted as a crane, was said to have landed on the Primeval Mound as the sun's rays lit the earth when it emerged from the annual Nile flood.*

118 Re-Herakhty, Horus-of-the-Horizon, was another aspect of the sun deity. The hawk-headed god wears the Atef-crown (like Osiris in ill. 112), with its characteristic sun-disc in the centre and plumes on either side.

(Below right)

119 (Above) The dawn or rising sun was often depicted as Khepri, the dung beetle, pushing its ball of dung out of which, the Egyptians mistakenly believed, its offspring emerged as the sun emerges from the eastern horizon. (Centre) The evening sun, or the sun at night, was seen in the ram-headed god carrying a sceptre. (Below) The solar boat, here shown in a stylized hieroglyph, almost always had a curious rectangular object hanging off the bow – perhaps representing the Field of Reeds through which the boat passed.

tary; at one point, thoroughly humbled, the King of Upper and Lower Egypt pleads for a position as the little pygmy who dances 'to entertain the heart of the god'. In one horrific passage, the king becomes a cannibal, devouring all the gods and concentrating their powers into himself as the supreme deity.

The Texts as we know them were compiled by the priesthood of Heliopolis, now a suburb on the northern fringes of Cairo but in ancient times the centre of the cult of the Sun-god and the seat of the sacred *benben*. The *benben* was a cult object, probably of stone, shaped like a small pyramid or pyramidion and representing the Primeval Hill, the first part of the earth in creation mythology to have emerged from the watery chaos, just as the black earth of Egypt emerged each year as the Nile flood waters began to subside. The pyramids probably derived their shape (but not of course their cumulative mass) from the *benben*, as did almost certainly the obelisk, a later development. It was on the Primeval Hill of the *benben* that the Sun-god first revealed himself in the shape of the phoenix bird. In other forms the god manifested himself as Horus, the hawk, soaring the heavens; as Khepri, the scarab beetle, pushing a ball of dung out of

which, the Egyptians mistakenly thought, the beetle's offspring emerged as the sun emerges each morning; as the Atum, the actual disc of the sun itself, especially at midday; and, in a fusion of two manifestations, as Re-

118   Herakhty, the hawk on the horizon. Although they are at first confusing, these different names and manifestations all represent one great god. All were worshipped at Heliopolis (but not only at Heliopolis) and all were seen as simultaneous manifestations of the singular, immanent power of the unique god of the sun.

In whatever form he manifested himself, the Sun-god traversed the sky in a special boat, whose ritual shape and equipment remained much the same throughout Egyptian history. The Sun-god's boat was originally a papyrus raft and from this we can deduce that the cult of the Sun-god was very old indeed, going back certainly to a time before the Egyptians knew how to build boats out of wood. Miriam Lichtheim has translated Utterance 263, which she says is the oldest of the Pyramid Texts concerned with crossing the sky by boat:

> *The sky's reed-floats are launched for Re,*
> *That he may cross on them to lightland;*
> *The sky's reed-floats are launched for Herakhty,*
> *That Herakhty may cross on them to Re;*
> *The sky's reed-floats are launched for Unas,*
> *That he may cross on them to lightland, to Re;*
> *The sky's reed-floats are launched for Unas,*
> *That he may cross on them to Herakhty, to Re.*[2]

The reed-floats are a primitive kind of transport, probably nothing more than two big bundles of papyrus bound together. Later texts mention boats, and what is meant is almost certainly papyriform wooden boats. Sometimes the boat that crossed the daytime sky was said to be the same as that which made the more perilous journey beneath the world through the hours of darkness where the Apopis serpent lay in wait to swallow

XIII   the sun. At other times, it was said that the god possessed a daytime boat

129   as well as a night-time boat, the latter equipped with special offerings and magic charms to ward off the dangers and evils of the underworld.

The priesthood of Heliopolis was powerful enough to dominate the royal mortuary religion. But at some time before the Pyramid Texts were carved on the walls of King Unas' pyramid, the cult of Osiris had become sufficiently important that the Heliopolitan priests felt it necessary to incorporate large parts of the Osirian religion with the sun-cult.

We cannot say that the worship of Osiris is as old as that of the sun, although it seems likely that an agricultural society would worship a fer-

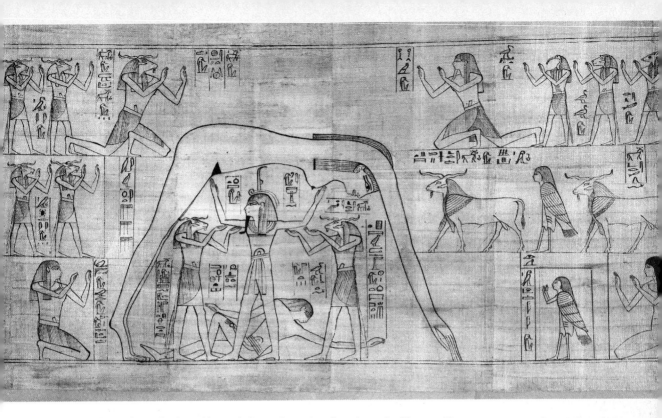

120 The body of Nut the sky-goddess arched over the earth to form the vault of heaven. She was sometimes said to swallow the sun-disc in the evening and expel it again each morning. Her husband Geb, the earth-god, reclines at her feet whilst her father, Shu, the god of air, supports her.

tility god. Small figures related to the cult of Osiris and his sister-consort Isis were found in predynastic graves, dating from before 3000 BC, at Helwan, on the east bank of the Nile opposite the ancient site of Memphis, but there is no evidence of anything earlier. Another early religious document, the Memphite Theology, a creation myth that some scholars believe may go back to the First Dynasty, recounts the death of Osiris and the subsequent succession of his son Horus, a mythological re-enactment of the death and succession of the king, indicating·that by the First Dynasty the legend was already well established.

Osiris, Seth and Isis (together with their sister Nephthys who played a minor role in the myth) were the offspring of Nut the goddess of the sky (whose arched body forms the vault of heaven over the reclining earth *120* in ancient portrayals) and the earth-god Geb. Geb had given dominion over the world to his first-born Osiris, but Seth, in a fit of jealousy, murdered his brother, drowning him in the Nile, or, in later texts, dismembering him and scattering his parts over Egypt. Isis rescued Osiris, and pulled his body ashore at Memphis. (In Plutarch's recounting, *De Iside et Osiride*, Isis journeyed to Byblos where she found Osiris' body in a tree trunk that had been cut down to make a pillar for the palace

of the prince of Byblos, but there is no trace of this interesting excursion in the earlier texts.) Fluttering her wings over his recumbent body, Isis reanimated Osiris sufficiently that she was able to conceive a son, Horus, *121* born in the reed marshes of the Delta where some scholars suggest the Osiris legend originated. After his reanimation, Osiris became king of *112* the dead. Horus, legitimate heir to Osiris' earthly dominion, determined to avenge his father, and after a terrible struggle with his uncle, during which Seth plucked out one of his nephew's eyes (the eyes of Horus the falcon-god were said to be the sun and the moon), Seth was vanquished and the victorious Horus succeeded to his father's throne, his eye restored by the intervention of the moon-god Thoth. In the words of the Memphite Theology: 'Horus appeared as King of Upper Egypt and appeared as King of Lower Egypt in the embrace of his father Osiris [that is, probably in the *ka*-embrace that would transfer to Horus the vital divine and royal force of Osiris] together with the gods who were in front of him and who were behind him.'³

In primitive agricultural societies, the institution of kingship is closely connected with the fertility of the soil. It may be, as some scholars have suggested, that when the king's power was seen to be waning, that is, when crops failed or in their natural season died off, the king was killed and buried in the earth, that his remaining power might contribute to a new season's growth. It is a myth from the deepest origins of human culture. Certainly there is no suggestion that such dark events took place during Egypt's historical period, but the *hebsed* festival, with a ritual race run round a court such as the *hebsed* court at King Zoser's pyramid at *12* Saqqara, seems to have been a ceremony designed to rejuvenate symbolically the king's flagging power. By the time the Egyptians entered on the stage of history, they had already evolved a higher philosophy than that of the simple corn-god, but we can still trace, in the Egyptian notion of kingship, elements of a more primitive fertility cult.

Curiously, however, the original fertility god, Osiris, is the dead king, and it is his son, Horus, who is the living king, guarantor of *ma'et*, the order of the universe on which depended the fertility of men, animals and agriculture. Horus, whether in the Osiris legend or as the falcon-god of the sun, bears no trace of an origin in the cult of a vegetation god. He is a warrior, pure and simple, who avenges his father's murder and defends his rightful inheritance, Egypt.

Horus the living king becomes Osiris the dead king who is succeeded by Horus the living king in an unchanging cycle. Professor Frankfort claimed that the Egyptian word *ḥm*, commonly translated 'majesty' as in the sense of 'Your Majesty', should in fact be translated as 'incarnation' or 'embodiment'. Thus the god's power or *ka* would be temporarily

(Opposite)
121 Horus the child (Harpocrates) is indicated by the side curl of hair which was the traditional symbol of childhood in ancient Egypt. The divine figure of Horus is deeply embedded in many conflicting Egyptian mythologies, as the falconer hawk-god of the heavens, as the god of the sun and as the royal avenger of his father Osiris. In this image he is seen emerging from the protection of his mother Isis.

122 manifest in the person of Cheops or Djedefre or Chephren, but the individuals themselves were successive incarnations of one god. I do not know whether this theory can be sustained or not, but it does provide an interesting insight into the notion of a kingship that is as unchanging and perpetual as the notion of *ma'et*.

The pyramids themselves were obviously a reflection of the cult of the Sun-god, but I have dealt at some length with the Osiris legend because by the time of the Pyramid Age, the two cults had interpenetrated in Egyptian thought about the afterlife. We can see this interpenetration in the cosmogony of the Great Ennead, the nine great gods, which began with Atum, the sun, as creator and prime mover. Atum engendered Shu (air) and Tefnut (moisture) and from this couple came Geb and Nut, earth and sky, who were, as we have seen, the parents of Osiris, Isis, Seth and Nephthys. Osiris was worshipped chiefly at Abydos where the Great Procession was an annual event that attracted pilgrims from all over Egypt. They came by boat, and their boats were usually some derivation of the papyriform craft of the Sun-god. Re-Atum was worshipped in many places in his many manifestations, especially in later history, but Heliopolis remained the centre of orthodox theology, the Rome of the Egyptian world. Increasingly the Osiris cult came to dominate the religious thinking of the Egyptians, but the sun-cult too remained important. Long after the end of the Old Kingdom, Amon, a local god of Thebes, became Amon-Re, god of the sun and supreme god of Egypt, and the cult of the sun really became what amounted to an official state religion. But that is all later Egyptian history and need not concern us here.

The religion of the ancient Egyptians is a complex and difficult subject, partly by its very nature, with its great pantheon of gods and goddesses and its apparently conflicting statements about the relationships of gods and men in the universe, and partly because our own thought processes are so very different. We can look upon the Egyptians as people in a pre-logical state, who simply did not understand that mutually exclusive propositions could not be true at one and the same time. Or we can view them as people gifted with an insight that we have since lost – that truth, as a philosophical or scientific or moral statement, is not exclusive but rather inclusive and all-embracing.

I have tried in this discussion to stay away from the more controversial problems of Egyptian religion. Much has been written about the subject, and much of that, unfortunately, has been nonsense. I wanted to give instead a brief survey of Egyptian attitudes towards death and the afterlife and the role of the king therein, during the period of the Old Kingdom, so that the reader will at least have some guidance in the chapter that follows.

(Opposite)

122 Horus as the protector of the king holds Chephren in his embrace, both transmitting and preserving the royal power. This is another view of the magnificent diorite statue first seen in ill. 18.

123 *A model of the Royal Ship, built by Ahmed Youssef Moustafa. Although the canopy in the model has been extended to the baldachin, in the actual reconstruction the two do not touch and the baldachin is much farther forward.*

CHAPTER EIGHT

Conclusion

Why did the Egyptians build an enormous, forty-three-metre-long wooden ship to simulate a humble raft of bound bundles of papyrus? And, having done so, why did they then proceed to dismantle the ship and bury it for eternity in the pit next to the pyramid?

The answers to these questions seem to lie in that most ancient and enduring Egyptian myth, the journey of the Sun-god around the heavens in his Reed Float. Papyriform boats were built in a deliberate imitation of the Sun-god's raft, and in the earliest depictions that we know, the shape of the Sun-god's vessel closely resembles that of the Royal Ship. Even as late as the Twenty-sixth Dynasty, the sun-boat, painted piously on coffins and papyrus texts, although it was often subject to artistic variations, continued to look very much like Cheops' great craft.

The Sun-god travelled by boat, because that was virtually the only method of transport known to the Egyptians, at least in the Old Kingdom. And he travelled in a raft of bound papyrus presumably because the myth was so old that it antedated a time when the Egyptians knew about and could build wooden ships. The papyrus raft then gained a certain religious significance by association with the Sun-god, and it maintained that significance despite its more practical and prosaic functions. But reed perishes quickly, as the Egyptians, constantly repairing and rebuilding their marsh boats, knew well. For the hereafter a more enduring material was needed. Wood, especially Lebanese cedarwood, was not only peculiarly long-lasting, but it was also imbued with a sacred and royal significance that made it the ideal material for the king's imperishable Reed Float, a duplicate of that of the Sun-god.

To say that the king's papyriform boat duplicated the Sun-god's is not to say that they had the same functions. At this stage of our knowledge about the Old Kingdom, the question of why this magnificent cedar vessel was buried next to Cheops' Great Pyramid cannot be answered for certain, though any number of assertions have been and will continue to be made.

Nothing else quite like the Royal Ship has ever been found. The Dahshur boats, which are the closest thing to it, were assumed by their excava- *100, 101* tor to have been part of the burial equipment of King Sesostris III, but recently serious doubts have been raised as to whether they have any connection at all with that important Twelfth Dynasty king. They are in any case hardly of the scale or elegance or magnificence of the Royal Ship.

Boat-graves, which we assume once held actual boats (but did they always?), occur as far as we know at only two periods in Egyptian history: during the Archaic Period of the First and Second Dynasties in the royal graves at Saqqara and in the necropolis of the nobles across the river at Helwan; and during the Fourth Dynasty, primarily at Giza, with the exception of Djedefre's boat-pit next to his pyramid at Abu Roash. (But the pyramid at Abu Roash may have been intended by its builder to define the northern limits of an eventual pyramid field that would begin with Cheops' Great Pyramid at Giza.) At the end of the Fifth Dynasty or the beginning of the Sixth Dynasty King Unas had two boat-pits, each about fifty metres long and lined in white Tura limestone, dug in the bedrock to the south of the fine covered Causeway that led from his Saqqara pyramid to its Valley Temple. Except for these, and the Twelfth Dynasty boats that may have belonged to Sesostris III, we know of no other boat-pits after the close of the Fourth Dynasty.★

It is altogether possible that boat-pits were a continuous tradition from the First Dynasty right up to the reign of King Unas or even later, and that we have either not found most of them or that evidence of them has been destroyed in previous excavations. But there are significant differences between the early Archaic boat-pits and the later ones of the Fourth Dynasty that make me think we are possibly seeing two different traditions.

In the first place, each of the earlier boat-pits was located to the north of a grave. (The few exceptions to this rule may well prove on examination to be mistaken attributions that should in fact be thought of as belonging to graves that are to the south of the boat-pits concerned.) Another difference of possible significance is that the Archaic Period boat-pits seem always to have been single pits connected each with an individual grave. In the Fourth Dynasty, on the other hand, we often have groups of boat-pits located on several sides of the pyramid grave and not restricted to the north alone.

Most, perhaps all, of the Fourth Dynasty boat-graves are connected with reigning monarchs. Although the Archaic boat-pits at Saqqara seem

---

★ Another construction frequently mentioned along with boat-graves is the 'solar barque' of King Niuserre in the Fifth Dynasty. It was a model boat built of mud-brick south of the sun temple constructed by this king near Abusir, but as it was unconnected with his pyramid or his burial, I feel it has no part in the present discussion.

124 Painted on a limestone block near the pyramid of Mycerinus at Giza, this boat hieroglyph is thought by some archaeologists to indicate the presence of at least one boat-pit in association with this pyramid.

also to have been connected with royal graves, it is not at all clear whether the graves at Helwan were of royalty only, or of the nobility and other citizens as well. The excavator, Zaki Saad, certainly believed that the Helwan burials were not exclusively royal.

In the Fourth Dynasty, Cheops had five boat-pits that we presently know of, Chephren possibly had six, and at the pyramid of Mycerinus, the smallest of the three Giza pyramids, a boat hieroglyph has been found *124* that some archaeologists believe may indicate the presence of at least one boat-grave here as well. Several small boat-pits seem to belong to the subsidiary pyramids next to the Great Pyramid. These little pyramids are *14* traditionally ascribed to Cheops' principal queens, but there is not a great deal of evidence to support the assertion. Egyptian custom generally provided for only one Great Queen, usually, as we have seen, the eldest daughter of the previous ruler, though a king might have several wives in addition to his concubines. It seems odd that Cheops would have had three principal queens. Perhaps these pyramids had some other function in the royal burial scheme.

At the end of the dynasty Queen Khentkawes had a boat-pit on the southwest corner of her most peculiar grave, neither pyramid nor mastaba, near the Sphinx at Giza, but a good argument can be made that Khentkawes was a reigning monarch herself, the last ruler of the Fourth Dynasty, despite the fact that she was a woman. Djedefre, of course, had only one boat-pit that we know of, but his pyramid complex is in such a ruinous condition that there may very well have been others which have since disappeared.

There are then these significant differences between the Archaic Period boat-graves and those of the Fourth Dynasty: their location in relation to the graves; the number of pits attached to a grave; and the presence or absence of a royal connection. The early Saqqara boat-pits are also a good deal smaller than the later ones, averaging between ten and fifteen metres long, with none longer than twenty metres. What are we to make of this? Is it possible, as has been suggested, that the Archaic boat-burials, situated to the north of the graves, have to do with a stellar cult, one that was always present to a greater or lesser degree in Egyptian religion but that seems to have been strongest just before the dynastic period, when it was taken over, absorbed into the cults of Osiris and of the Sun-god? Many (although not all) Egyptologists feel that the very earliest Utterances in the Pyramid Texts reflect this belief in a stellar cult that would require the deceased to journey to the stars or to join in an afterlife circuit of the pole star, eternally wheeling, by boat of course, around this fixed northern point.

I have not dealt much in the previous chapter with the stellar aspects of Egyptian religion, because it is not really relevant to the Pyramid Age with which we have been dealing. I noted earlier that the stars were sometimes thought of as *ba*s, the bird-souls of the deceased. The Egyptians also sometimes described their dead kings as having ascended to the stars, particularly to the stars that revolved eternally around the pole star. These circumpolar stars were called in the Pyramid Texts the Indestructible Stars or the Imperishable Stars. By the beginning of the dynastic period, the stellar cult is believed to have diminished from its earlier importance, but perhaps the northern location of the early boat-pits reflects a lingering tradition. Certainly the northern placement of the entrance to the pyramids, which continued right through the Pyramid Age, reflects beliefs connected with the earlier cult. Rather than entrance, we should perhaps think of it as an exit, the passage for the king's spirit to the stars.

If the earlier boats were intended to transport the deceased to the stars, were the Fourth Dynasty boats, then, reflecting the predominance at that time of the solar cult, meant to carry the dead king on his journey with the Sun-god? It is an answer that is often given and that is argued forcefully by Kamal el-Mallakh, the discoverer of the boat-pits, who has referred to the Royal Ship as a 'solar barque' from the very beginning. Mallakh believes that the reconstructed Royal Ship represents the *m'nḏt*, the boat in which the Sun-god crosses the daytime sky. The second, unopened boat-pit on the pyramid's south face, he feels, will be found to contain the night-time boat, the *mskt.t*, which, in keeping with the more perilous nature of the night journey, will be accompanied by offerings to ward off the dangers of the night.

Other archaeologists and Egyptologists have pointed out that the Sun-god has a boat of his own already. The dead king was said to travel in that boat and would therefore, to the literal-minded Egyptians, have no need for another boat at all, at least as far as his solar journeys were concerned. Moreover, they argue, none of the attributes that are traditionally found accompanying the solar barque were found in the pit. These attributes vary considerably: they might be the ram-headed or hawk-headed figure of the Sun-god himself; or the disc of the sun, the Atum; *119* or the Khepri dung-beetle; or the steps that may represent a ladder to heaven and that many Egyptologists believe is the origin of the form of the Step Pyramid; or the curious blade-like instrument that is sometimes called an executioner's knife. One or several of these attributes is always present to signify that a papyriform boat is in fact a solar barque and not an ordinary funerary or pilgrimage boat. Another typical feature of the solar barque is a strange rectangular mat or fringe that hangs off the bow *119* post and that appears to be made of woven reeds, perhaps in a symbolic reference to the Field or Marsh of Reeds through which the sun-boat passes before it emerges at dawn. The boat of the Sun-god is never shown with either sails or oars, though usually it has two or more steering-oars slung off the after deck. Being divine, it needs no human or other propulsion. Not one of these devices, as we have seen, was included with the Royal Ship, and of course the very presence of the five pairs of oars, symbolic though their function may have been, is an argument against the solar barque.

Ahmed Youssef Moustafa is convinced that the Royal Ship was not intended as a symbolic means of transport but was actually used – at least once, if not several times. He bases his judgment on evidence from the ship itself: across certain of the 'baffles', boomerang-shaped pieces of wood that were inserted to relieve the great strain of the rope bindings on the wood, as well as in other places, the wood was marked, scarred as it were, by the ropes which, in shrinking, had left a clear imprint *125* on the water-softened wood. Hag Ahmed calls the Royal Ship a 'funerary barque'. He believes that it was used perhaps only once, to transport the dead king's body in a solemn funeral procession from Memphis, the capital, down-river to the royal burial ground at Giza. We can see a similar kind of procession in a late papyrus, from the Twenty-first Dynasty, about 1000 BC, in the British Museum. Called 'The Book of *126* the Dead of Queen Nejmt', it shows precisely the same lines as the Royal Ship in a papyriform funerary barque that is being drawn on a sledge across the desert to the necropolis. (One recalls that the Dahshur boats had been found with the remnants of a sledge that had obviously been used for the same purpose, to pull the boats from the river's edge to the burying ground.) The mummy of the deceased queen – or of her consort, the High Priest of Amun – is presumably inside the cabin which looks astonishingly similar in construction to the cabin on the Royal Ship, although it lacks a canopy.

The Royal Ship, in its journey from Memphis to Giza, would have been towed by smaller craft, though it would have depended on the strong river current for its main propulsion. The priests and nobles and royal sons who manned the oars, including the two great steering-oars, would have been there for symbolic reasons as well as to help keep the ship on course. A witness to the stately procession would inevitably have been reminded of the passage in the Pyramid Texts referring to the ferrying of the dead king across the waters to the hereafter. Once again in Egyptian belief, actual and symbolic acts interpenetrate, enriching each other with both reality and magic.

Hag Ahmed believes that the Royal Ship was built on purpose as a funerary barque, that is, that it was not part of the royal fleet commandeered after the king's death for this sacred use. Papyriform boats are usually shown painted green amidships and yellow ochre at each end, with the all-seeing, all-protective *wedjat*-eye drawn on either side of the bow. Björn Landström, who is not an Egyptologist but who probably knows more about ancient Egyptian ships and ship-building than any person alive, detects in the fact that the Royal Ship's hull is unpainted and undecorated, evidence that the ship was built in a hurry – for a last pilgrimage, Landström speculates, carrying the king's mummy to the holy places of Egypt, Saïs, Buto and Abydos.

Dr Iskander, in charge of chemical restoration of the boat, would concur with the idea of a hasty construction, for he believes that the Royal Ship was actually built on the Giza plateau next to the already dug grave – built, dismantled and buried all in one operation. Dr Iskander's conclusion is based on the presence, in the mud plaster that covered the limestone blocks over the pit, of many sizeable pieces of cedar, acacia and other woods that had been used in the ship's construction, such as would have

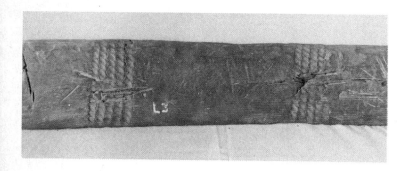

125 Hag Ahmed Youssef believes that the Royal Ship must have been used at least once, for only shrinking ropes pulled tautly across soft wet wood could have left such clear impressions as these on the seam battens inside the ship's hull.

126 A late papyrus, from the Twenty-first Dynasty, shows a boat similar to the Royal Ship being drawn on a sledge. The cabin, which bears a curious resemblance to that on Cheops' boat, encloses the coffin of Queen Nejmt (or of her husband, the High Priest of Amun) which is being borne to its resting place in the tomb. The Royal Ship, in similar fashion, may have borne the coffin of Cheops, drawn on a sledge up the Causeway to the Great Pyramid.

been left by boatwrights in the normal course of operation. The question that continues to puzzle is why the pit was so much shorter than the boat. The only sensible answer has to be that the ship's exact measurements for some reason were not available to the people who were excavating the pit, which would dispose of Dr Iskander's theory, but would still leave unexplained the carpentry debris left behind. I. E. S. Edwards, former Keeper of Egyptian Antiquities at the British Museum, takes a more cautious view. Assuming that all the boat-pits around Cheops' pyramid once contained actual boats, he suggests that some of the boats were used in the funeral ceremonies and processions, while others were intended 'to provide the dead king with a means of transport in his After-life'. The distinguished Egyptologist J. E. Černý supported this theory; the Royal Ship and her sister, he felt, were for the eastern and western voyaging of the dead king, while the empty pits on the east face of the pyramid probably once contained the boats for the northern and southern journeys, and the now empty pit next to the Causeway the king's actual funerary barge.

Throughout Egyptian history, the use of papyriform boats seems to have been restricted to events that had a religious or cultic significance – as pilgrimage boats, for instance, especially to the important site of Abydos, sacred to Osiris, where every Egyptian hoped to journey if not annually, at least once in his lifetime; or as funerary boats, to transport the mummy across the river to the necropolis on the west bank; or as vehicles for the transport of important gods. In this last case, the religious significance was doubly emphasized, for in later times (and probably earlier as well) the image of the god – Amon, for instance – was exhibited in a papyriform barque, a fabulous vessel of gold encrusted with precious stones, never meant to be placed in the water but rather to be borne aloft

127 The wedjat-eye was often painted as a protective device on the bows of ships, particularly of papyriform craft. The absence of any decoration whatsoever on the Royal Ship suggests that she was constructed hastily.

on the shoulders of the priests or other members of the religious procession – and then to be placed in the seat of honour on an actual papyriform barge, gilded equally lavishly, which was floated across the Nile during the annual Feast of the Valley when Amon visited the holy places of Thebes.

We have seen that the sacred form most probably originated in the Reed Float of the Sun-god which was itself a throw-back to a time when the Egyptians knew virtually no other form of transport. Translated into the permanence of cedar, which had special connotations of immortality, it became the king's transport as well. It seems altogether possible that the king never travelled anywhere for any reason in anything but a papyriform boat. Like so many royal privileges, this one too could be offered to selected people whom the king wished to honour, in the same way that he might also offer them a statue for their tomb, or a piece of land the income from which would secure food and drink offerings for eternity. In this way, many of the mortuary rites and customs that had been restricted to royalty in the Old Kingdom had, before the Twelfth Dynasty (that is, *c.* 1900 BC), become privileges that were assumed to be rights of the noble classes. Later still, these same privileges of burial rite and equipment would become available to anyone who had the means to pay for them.

By the Twelfth Dynasty, the Pyramid Texts had also been adopted by the nobility and, with some changes and developments, painted on *130* the interiors of coffins – whence they derive their later name of Coffin Texts. Just as it was now too expensive to carve these spells on the walls

128 This unfinished relief in the Deir el-Bahri (Thebes) tomb of Nespekashuti dates from the seventh century BC and shows a papyriform pilgrimage boat, nearly 2000 years after the construction of Cheops' Royal Ship, being towed by another craft. The relief is labelled 'The Return from Abydos', the city sacred to Osiris to which every Egyptian hoped to make the pilgrimage at least once in his lifetime.

129 *The night boat of the sun, in a preliminary drawing for an unfinished relief carving in the Eighteenth Dynasty tomb of Horemhab. The ram-headed Sun-god is protected by two serpents, within and without the shrine.*

of tombs, so no one could afford to bury actual boats with the deceased. The custom then grew up of placing models in the tombs – a delightful custom that has granted us an extremely privileged look at daily life in ancient Egypt – charming models of carpenters' shops, of potters' studios, of laundries, bakeries, butchers, and many, many models of boats. Already around 2000 BC the nobleman Meketre was buried at Thebes with a dozen of these model boats, and we must believe that these represented exact replicas of the little fleet that a man of Meketre's standing would have maintained in real life. There were four travelling boats, two under sail and two to be rowed, two kitchen tenders to accompany the travelling boats on voyages and provide for the crew as well as passengers, and four papyriform 'yachts', to use their excavator's terminology, looking very much like miniatures of King Cheops' Royal Ship.[1] Painted green and ochre, these must have represented Meketre's pilgrimage and funerary vessels, to enable him to continue 'on the celestial Nile' the voyages he had made in his lifetime. Not all Egyptians, by any means, could have

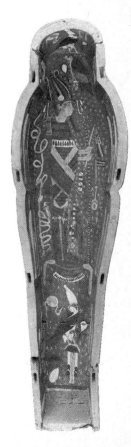

131

130 *The serpent is both protector and adversary. Here Osiris, on a painted coffin cover, lies in the starry underworld, guarded by the serpent. But the serpent must be defeated before Osiris can be resurrected, and the Dragon of Darkness, Apopis, must be overcome before the sun's boat can emerge into the new dawn.*

maintained such a fleet, but almost all Egyptians would have needed a papyriform pilgrimage and burial boat. Those who could not afford a special vessel reserved for this purpose would perhaps, as we have speculated, have added papyriform stem and stern pieces to an ordinary travelling boat, and it seems quite possible that these would have been socketed on in precisely the same way the stem and stern pieces are socketed on to the Royal Ship.

106, 107, XII   It has been suggested that the Royal Ship is part of just such a flotilla, on a grander scale, as the model one buried with Meketre. In Cheops' case they could have been either ships used in his lifetime or special ones constructed for his burial equipment. They may have been used to carry to the pyramid his mummy in its coffin, his mummified viscera, perhaps in an alabaster container like that of Queen Hetep-heres, and all the royal funerary paraphernalia, burial equipment and offerings for his happiness and well-being in the afterlife. The boats were then buried for the king's use in eternity.

The Royal Ship today

The Royal Ship of King Cheops is the oldest, the largest and the best-preserved of any ancient ship that has ever been found, an extraordinary testimony to the technological skill of the ancient Egyptians and a precious clue to the origins of maritime history. It is all the more a pity, then, that this unique find, so carefully and intelligently restored by Ahmed Youssef Moustafa, should be left virtually exposed to the elements in a museum that is at best inadequate and at worst a downright threat to the ship's survival. 'The wooden parts of the boat', wrote the late Dr Abdel Moneim Abubakr in 1971, 'were as hard and new as if they had been placed there but a year ago.' Kamal el-Mallakh recalls that when he opened the pit in 1954 the original colour of the wood was warm and light and 'so highly polished that I could sometimes see my own reflection in a piece of side planking'. These statements, unfortunately, are no longer true. Despite all the attention that continues to be given to the boat, principally by Hag Ahmed Youssef who maintains a constant check on the condition of the ancient timbers, the ship will not be safe until it is decently housed, and protected from temperature and humidity fluctuations as well as from the danger of fire, which would be disastrous on the nearly waterless desert plateau.

4, IV

132 View along the port side of the reconstructed Royal Ship towards the bow. The internal ropes stitching the ship together are just visible between the hull timbers, though originally none would have been seen from the outside.

Experts in the preservation of ancient wood agree that the ideal situation for the restored boat would be to duplicate as nearly as possible the conditions in the pit, conditions that preserved the ship nearly intact for some four and a half millennia. Even with the best air conditioning unit imaginable these conditions would be difficult to maintain in a glass house in the desert. The temperature in the pit was fairly constant at 22° Centigrade. The temperature in the museum is often more than twice that. But high temperatures and dry air are not in themselves such grave problems as are the fluctuations in temperature and humidity. Wood, even 4,500-year-old wood, is a natural living medium, reacting to its environment, expanding and contracting with heat and cold, moisture and dryness. Such continual changes, often taking place over a short period of time, strain these ancient timbers to the breaking point, and there is almost nothing that can be done to counteract them short of changing the environment in which the boat now rests.

It would seem to be a simple enough chore, to redesign the glass museum, or to build an entirely new museum, to house the Royal Ship in a worthy setting and a proper environment – simple, and not very costly when measured, for instance, against the amount of money that was spent to rescue the Nubian monuments threatened by the High Dam at Aswan. Money could certainly be found for such an important project, and goodwill too is not lacking, as Hag Ahmed has shown. But money and goodwill alone cannot solve the problem. Something more is needed. From the day of its discovery, the Royal Ship has been the victim of what inevitably appears to an outsider to be petty bureaucratic politicking and crude jockeying for public recognition. Individual pride and national honour help to confuse the problem: it is extremely difficult for the Egyptians to admit that a problem does exist and to accept the fact that foreign help, both financial and technological, will be necessary to solve it. The prospect of losing the boat through negligence and indifference is horrifying, but, to Egypt's shame, it is a very real possibility. What can be done to save it?

Probably the only way in the end to control what happens to the boat and to what is assumed to be the sister ship in the second pit is through the establishment of a national or better, even an international, commission, under Egyptian control but drawing freely on the expertise and experiences of the great number of maritime museums that have been established lately in Northern Europe and America. Such a commission must have an independent authority in order to distance itself as much as possible from the politicking that has dogged the boat in the past. And it would need financial independence sufficient to build and maintain a proper museum that would be large enough for both boats – and to make possible

(Opposite)

133 Looking up at the port side stern section – the majestic sweep of the ship is supported by a series of steel stanchions.

168

the excavation and restoration, under Hag Ahmed Youssef's supervision, of the sister craft.

But the problem is not with the boats alone. The entire Giza plateau, in fact the whole stretch of pyramid fields south at least as far as Saqqara, faces two threats: the expansion of the city of Cairo, whose population has more than trebled in the last dozen years, and the tourist boom that, with optimistic solutions in sight for Egypt's external political problems, has already begun on a mass scale. Even today an extension of the pyramid road leads up to the plateau itself, crosses right over the black basalt paving-stones of King Cheops' Mortuary Temple, and swings out between the two main pyramids towards 'Sahara City', a newly fashionable suburb, where unattractive bungalows mar the horizon, in full view of, and dominating, the sacred burial ground of Egypt's ancient kings. Under the aspect of eternity it is all a little ridiculous, a testament to modern folly and greed. Unfortunately it is likely to get much worse before it ever gets even slightly better. Already it is almost impossible to see the pyramids as Vivant Denon saw them when he came out with Napoleon in 1798, 'in that refined and transparent colouring they owe to the immense volume of air surrounding them. . . . The great distance from which they can be perceived makes them appear diaphanous, tinted with the bluish tone of the sky, and restores to them the perfection and purity of the angles which the centuries have marred.'[2] These days, from a great distance the pyramids too often cannot be perceived at all, owing to the industrial and automobile pollution that stains the air for miles around Cairo.

It has been proposed that the entire area surrounding the pyramids for several miles be ceded to the Department of Antiquities in perpetuity as archaeological territory. The existing settlement at Sahara City would be dismantled before it has a chance to swell any further, and the boundaries of 'Pacific Properties', a questionable venture into tourist development by a Hong Kong real-estate speculator, would be kept sufficiently far away to be invisible from the heights of the plateau. Admission to the pyramid area would be restricted to ticket-holders, and transportation by electric motor carts within the area would be under the supervision of the Department of Antiquities with no private vehicles allowed. The income thus accumulated (surprisingly no admission fee is presently charged at the Giza pyramids and at Saqqara the fee is minimal) would pay for guards, guides and maintenance of the monuments – including of course the Royal Ship – with a healthy sum left over to support further excavation and restoration. If it all sounds a little bit like Disneyland-on-the-Nile, one must remember that the alternative is uncontrolled development led by the worst kind of property speculators and corrupt and

(Opposite)

134 The papyriform stern section of the ship with the two steering oars.

unscrupulous politicians who will sell off bit by bit not only Egypt's heritage but also one of her major sources of income in the future.

Under this scheme the Royal Ship would be properly housed in a controlled and stabilized environment, and the second pit would be uncovered and its contents excavated and reconstructed under the supervision of Hag Ahmed Youssef. In the second boat-pit obviously lie answers to many of the questions that the first boat has raised. In a certain sense, the form as well as the function of the Royal Ship will never be fully understood until the second pit is opened. But it must not be opened until the first boat can be properly maintained. The Royal Ship was excavated and reconstructed with the most painstaking methods, with the wise, and indeed, loving attention of the men who were involved, Kamal el-Mallakh, Salah Osman who supervised the removal of the blocks, Zaki Nour, in charge of the pyramids region, Zaki Iskander, Abdel Moneim Abubakr, and of course Ahmed Youssef Moustafa. It is a pity that the Royal Ship has been left to fend for herself in the inappropriate environment of the glass museum; it would be a tragedy if this magnificent ritual vessel, having survived forty-five centuries with a minimum of damage, were to disappear, because of our negligence and indifference, within our own lifetimes.

135 Just two of the dozens of different knots that held together the various sections of the Royal Ship – and that, reconstructed in modern rope, continue to hold her together today.

136 *The Royal Ship today in the museum at Giza; the fans that stir the air and provide the only kind of temperature and humidity control can be seen along the balcony in the middle left of the picture.*

Acknowledgments

I am grateful to the following individuals for the help they gave me and the patient courtesy with which my questions were answered and my needs were met: to Mae Trad, librarian of that unique institution, the Chicago House Library in Luxor; to Dr Lionel Casson of New York University, probably the world's leading authority on ancient ships, ship-building and maritime trade; to Kamal el-Mallakh, Zaki Iskander and Labib Habachi, among the many Egyptologists in that country and elsewhere who so generously shared their memories of the discovery and reconstruction of the Royal Ship as well as their knowledge of ancient Egyptian civilization; and of course to Hag Ahmed Youssef Moustafa, whose profound understanding of every aspect of the Royal Ship's history and construction made it possible for this book to be written.

Special thanks are due to Dr William Ward of the American University of Beirut who introduced me to Egyptology many years ago; to Christine Sturken for her indefatigable efforts as translator, hostess and friend; and to my husband Loren Jenkins for his support and patience and undiminished enthusiasm.

Notes on the text

Chapter Two

1 For a spirited defence of this viewpoint, see Mendelssohn, K. *The Riddle of the Pyramids*, London 1974.
2 Edwards, I. E. S. *The Pyramids of Egypt*, Harmondsworth 1961, p. 96.
3 Herodotus, *The Histories*, Book Two, 122 ff., transl. Aubrey de Selincourt, revised by A. R. Burn, Harmondsworth 1972.

Chapter Six

1 Transl. John A. Wilson, in Pritchard, J. B., ed. *Ancient Near Eastern Texts*, 3rd edn, Princeton 1969.
2 Ward, W. A., *Egypt and the East Mediterranean World*, Beirut 1971.
3 Transl. H. Goedicke, in *Journal of the American Research Center in Egypt*, 6 (1967), 93 ff., quoted in Ward, op. cit.
4 If, in fact, it was ever completely broken; see Ward, op. cit., for a discussion of continuing trade throughout the First Intermediate Period.
5 Of course there were many, many local differences. For an interesting survey of differences and similarities in early times see Baumgartel, E. *The Cultures of Prehistoric Egypt*, vols. I and II, London 1955 and 1960.
6 See note 5 above.
7 Herodotus, *The Histories*, Book Two, para. 96, transl. Lionel Casson (unpubl.). Although Herodotus speaks of a keel, Egyptian ships were flat-bottomed and keelless at least until well after the Middle Kingdom.

Chapter Seven

1 Lichtheim, M. *Ancient Egyptian Literature*, vol. I, *The Old and Middle Kingdom*, Berkeley 1975.
2 Lichtheim, op. cit.
3 Transl. John A. Wilson, in Pritchard (ed.) op. cit.
4 Frankfort, H. *Kingship and the Gods*, Chicago 1948, p. 45.

Chapter Eight

1 See Winlock, H. E. *Models of Daily Life in Ancient Egypt*, Cambridge, Mass. 1955.
2 Quoted in Herold, J. C. *Bonaparte in Egypt*, New York and London 1962.

Select bibliography

The abbreviation *ASAE* refers to the *Annales du Service des Antiquités en Égypte*.

ABUBAKR, A. M. and MOUSTAFA, A. Y. 'The Funerary Boat of Khufu', *Beiträge zur Ägyptischen Bauforschung und Altertumskunde*, 12 (1971), 1–18.

ALDRED, C. *Egypt to the End of the Old Kingdom*, London and New York 1965.

BAUMGARTEL, E. J. *The Cultures of Prehistoric Egypt*, vol. I, London 1955; vol. II, London 1960.

BLACKMAN, A. M. *The Rock Tombs of Meir*, vols. I–IV, London 1914–24.

BREASTED, J. H. *The Dawn of Conscience*, New York 1968.

BUTZER, K. W. 'Archaeology and Geology in Ancient Egypt', *Science*, 132 (1960), 167 ff.

CAPART, J. *Memphis*, Brussels 1930.

CASSON, L. *The Ancient Mariners*, London and New York 1959.

— *Ships and Seamanship in the Ancient World*, Princeton 1971.

ČERNÝ, J. 'A Note on the Recently Discovered Boat of Cheops', *Journal of Egyptian Archaeology*, 41 (1955), 75 ff.

DUNHAM, D. *The Egyptian Department and its Excavations*, Boston 1958.

EDWARDS, I. E. S. *The Pyramids of Egypt*, rev. edn, Harmondsworth and New York 1961.

EMERY, W. B. *The Tomb of Hemaka*, Cairo 1938.

— *The Tomb of Hor-Aha*, Cairo 1939.

— *Great Tombs of the First Dynasty*, vol. III, Cairo and London 1958.

FAGAN, B. M. *The Rape of the Nile*, New York 1976, London 1977.

FAKHRY, A. 'The Stela of the Boat-Captain Inikaf', *ASAE*, 38 (1938), 35 ff.

— *The Pyramids*, rev. edn, Chicago 1969.

FAULKNER, R. O. *The Ancient Egyptian Pyramid Texts*, Oxford 1969.

FRANKFORT, H. *Kingship and the Gods*, Chicago and London 1948.

GARDINER, A. H. *Egypt of the Pharaohs*, Oxford 1966.

— *Egyptian Grammar*, 3rd edn, Oxford 1973.

GASTER, T. H. *Thespis*, New York 1975.

GLANVILLE, S. R. K. *Catalogue of Egyptian Antiquities in the British Museum*, vol. II, *Wooden Model Boats*, rev. and completed by R. O. Faulkner, London 1972.

GREENHILL, B. *Archaeology of the Boat*, London and Middletown, Conn. 1976.

HASSAN, S. *Excavations at Giza*, 10 vols., Oxford and Cairo 1932–60.

HELCK, W. 'Die Handwerker- und Priesterphylen des Alten Reiches in Ägypten', *Die Welt des Orients*, VII (1973–74), 1–8.

HERODOTUS, *The Histories*, transl. Aubrey de Selincourt, rev. by A. R. Burn, Harmondsworth 1972.

HEROLD, J. C. *Bonaparte in Egypt*, New York and London 1962.

JEQUIER, G. *Les Pyramides des reines Neit et Apouit*, Cairo 1933.

JOHNSTONE, P. *The Archaeology of Ships*, London 1974.

KLEBS, G. *Die Relief des Altenreiches*, Heidelberg 1915.

LANDSTRÖM, B. *Ships of the Pharaohs*, Garden City, N.Y. and London 1970.

LAUER, J.-P. *Le Problème des pyramides*, Paris 1952.

LAUER, J.-P. *Saqqara*, London and New York 1976.

LICHTHEIM, M. *Ancient Egyptian Literature*, vol. I, *The Old and Middle Kingdom*, Berkeley 1975.

LUCAS, A. *Ancient Egyptian Materials and Industries*, 4th edn, rev. by J. R. Harris, London 1962.

MARAGIOGLIO, V. and RINALDI, C. *L'Architettura delle Piramidi Menfite*, Rome and Rapallo 1965.

MENDELSSOHN, K. *The Riddle of the Pyramids*, London and New York 1974.

MERCER, S. A. B. *The Pyramid Texts*, New York 1952.

MOUSTAFA, A. Y. 'Reparation and restoration of antiques', *ASAE*, 47 (1947), 77–95.

NOUR, M. Z., OSMAN, M. S., ISKANDER, Z. and MOUSTAFA, A. Y. *The Cheops Boats*, part I, Cairo 1960.

PETRIE, W. M. F. *Medum*, London 1892.

POSENER, G. *De la Divinité du pharaon*, Paris 1960.

PRITCHARD, J. B., ed. *Ancient Near Eastern Texts*, 3rd edn, Princeton 1969.

REISNER, G. A. *Models of Ships and Boats*, Cairo 1913.

— *The Development of the Egyptian Tomb down to the Accession of Cheops*, Cambridge, Mass. 1936.

REISNER, G. A. and SMITH, W. S. *A History of the Giza Necropolis*, vol. II, *The Tomb of Hetepheres, the Mother of Cheops*, Cambridge, Mass. 1955.

RUNDLE CLARK, R. T. *Myth and Symbol in Ancient Egypt*, London 1959 (reprinted 1978).

SAAD, Z. *Royal Excavations at Saqqara and Helwan (1941–45) ASAE*, supplément, cahier 3, Cairo 1947.

— *Royal Excavations at Helwan*, *ASAE*, supplément, cahier 14, Cairo 1951.

— *Excavations at Helwan*, Norman, Oklahoma 1969.

SERVIN, A. 'Constructions navales égyptiennes: Les barques de papyrus', *ASAE*, 48 (1949), 55–88.

SIMPSON, W. K. *The Literature of Ancient Egypt*, New Haven and London 1973.

SMITH, W. S. *Ancient Egypt as represented in the Museum of Fine Arts*, Boston 1960.

— *The Art and Architecture of Ancient Egypt*, Harmondsworth 1965.

WARD, W. A. *Egypt and the East Mediterranean World*, Beirut 1971.

WILSON, J. A. *The Culture of Ancient Egypt*, Chicago and London 1971.

WINLOCK, H. E. *Models of Daily Life in Ancient Egypt*, Cambridge, Mass. 1955.

List of illustrations

Index

Numerals in *italics* refer to illustration numbers